Publishing in Africa:
One Man's Perspective

Bellagio Studies in Publishing

Other titles in this series include:

Number 1: Philip G. Altbach, editor, *Publishing in Africa and the Third World*

Number 2: Carol Priestley, *Publishing Assistance Programs: Review and Inventory*

Number 3: Philip G. Altbach and Hyaeweol Choi, *Bibliography on Publishing in the Third World, 1980-1993* (Published by Ablex Publishers, 355 Chestnut St., Norwood, NJ 07648 USA)

Number 4: Philip G. Altbach, editor, *Copyright and Development: Inequality in the Information Age*

Number 5: Urvashi Butalia and Ritu Menon, *Making a Difference: Feminist Publishing in the South*

Publishing in Africa:
One Man's Perspective

Henry Chakava

Bellagio Studies in Publishing, 6

Bellagio Publishing Network
Research and Information Center
in association with the Boston College
Center for International Higher Education

Copublished with East African Educational Publishers, Ltd.
Nairobi, Kenya

Copublished with
East African Educational Publishers, Ltd.
Brick Court, Mpaka Road/Woodvale Grove
Westlands, P. O. Box 45314
Nairobi, Kenya

Bellagio Studies in Publishing books are distributed by the African Books Collective, Ltd.

© 1996 Bellagio Publishing Network and Henry Chakava

Copies of this book may be ordered from
African Books Collective, Ltd.
The Jam Factory
27 Park End St.
Oxford OX1 1HU, UK
Fax: 44-1865-793298

ISBN 0-9646078-1-6

ISBN number for Kenyan edition: 9966-46-669-X

CONTENTS

Preface	Philip G. Altbach	ix
Acknowledgements		xii
Foreword	Chinua Achebe	xiii

Introduction — 1

1. Kenyan Publishing: Independence and Dependence — 5

2. Private Enterprise Publishing in Kenya: A Long Struggle for Emancipation — 45

3. Publishing Ngugi: The Challenge, the Risk, and the Reward — 55

4. An Autonomous African Publishing House: A Model — 65

5. International Copyright and Africa: The Unequal Exchange — 75

6. Reading in Africa: Some Obstacles — 95

7. Book Marketing and Distribution: The Achilles Heel of African Publishing — 109

8. Pricing Publications — 135

Notes — 145

Appendixes

1. An Indigenous African Book Publishing Industry: In Search of a New Beginning — 149

2. Publishing and State Censorship in Kenya — 157

3. Reading Promotion in South Saharan Africa 163

4. The World Bank and African Publishing 171

5. The African Publishers' Network 177

Preface

Henry Chakava is one of Africa's most respected publishers. He is also a person who has a real commitment to books and to the role of the book in education and culture—for him, publishing is not just a commercial enterprise—it is a calling. Indeed, for publishers who work in the often difficult economic and political circumstances of Africa, publishing is more than a means of earning a living. It is a commitment to a broader set of values and concerns. This book shows the complex combination of issues that necessarily affect book publishing in Africa—and in developing countries generally. Henry Chakava writes about such diverse issues as copyright, book distribution, regional cooperation, autonomy and the problems of creating an independent publishing house in Africa, literacy and reading, and problems of censorship. It is unlikely that one of Chakava's Western colleagues would write about such a diversity of issues.

The world of publishing that Henry Chakava writes about in this book differs significantly from the debates about mergers and acquisitions, links between books and the entertainment industry, and the megadeals of New York or London. Yet, the West has an increasing influence on publishing in Africa and the Third World. As Chakava points out, the multinationals have immense power, and some of them have traditional links to Africa. In Francophone Africa, French publishers continue to dominate. The situation is more complex in Anglophone Africa, and indigenous publishers, such as Henry Chakava, have been able to achieve a measure of success. Today, in South Africa, the largest economy in the region and a major publishing center, major multinational publishers are increasingly influential, and many of the indigenous publishers who supported the liberal movement are severely threatened. Emerging African publishers will be confronted by trends in international publishing, and by multinationals wishing to enter the African market. As African publishing grows and shows potential, the multinationals will seek to dominate. It is a paradox that indigenous publishers will be left alone as long as they are unsuccessful. Once market potential has been demonstrated, outside pressures become evident.

Similarly, international trends in copyright, technology transfer, and in other areas are of increasing importance to Africa. As Henry

Chakava points out in this book, the international copyright system is highly unequal. There is little understanding among those in the industrialized world who control the system of the needs of emerging publishing industries and of the users of knowledge in developing countries. While Africa today has only limited access to such new technologies as computer-based knowledge networks, the World Wide Web, and similar innovations, the time is not too distant when publishers will be faced with dramatic technological challenges. As with copyright, these new technologies are controlled by corporations in the industrialized nations, and Africa will be forced to deal with those who control the system from a position of weakness.

There are many distinctly African problems facing publishing. Some of these challenges are discussed in this book. The problem of censorship and government repression is widespread, and certainly inhibits publishing. Sometimes, publishing a book is an act not only of economic uncertainty but of political and personal risk. Continuing difficulties of regional trade, currency instability and fluctuation, and sometimes high taxes on needed imports all cause problems for publishing and book distribution. Corruption at all levels of society is also a problem.

All, however, is not bleak. On the contrary, as Henry Chakava and his colleagues in organizations such as the African Publishers' Network (APNET) have shown, it is possible to establish successful publishing enterprises even in difficult circumstances. A commitment to the written word, to the role of the book in educational and cultural development, and the desire to build a successful business enterprise all contribute to the motivation of indigenous publishers.

The Bellagio Publishing Network Research and Information Center is pleased to publish this book. Our goal is to stimulate research on issues relating to publishing in Africa and the Third World and to disseminate information about trends, issues, and programs. This book will provide a unique perspective on African publishing from one of the continent's most experienced and respected publishers. Henry Chakava has been involved with the Bellagio Publishing Network from the beginning, and has been instrumental in bringing together African publishers, and colleagues from foundations, governments and others in the industrialized world who have a commitment to indigenous publishing in a creative dialogue. The Bellagio Publishing Network has been able to support several important initiatives, including APNET and the African Books Collective. Indeed, this volume is copublished by the Bellagio Network and East African Educational Publishers. It is distributed by the African Books Collective. In this way, this volume is an excellent example of the kind of collaboration that the Bellagio Publishing Network seeks to foster.

PHILIP G. ALTBACH

Acknowledgments

The chapters in this volume are reprinted from several sources. We acknowledge the following publications:

Chapter 1. From P. G. Altbach, ed., *Publishing and Development in the Third World* (1992), pp. 119–50. © 1992. Reprinted with the permission of Hans Zell Publishers, an imprint of Bowker-Saur, a division of Reed Elsevier (U.K.) Ltd.

Chapter 2. From *Logos* vol. 4, no. 3 (1993), pp. 130-35. © 1993. Reprinted with the permission of Whurr Publishers.

Chapter 3. From the *African Publishing Review* vol. 3, no. 4 (July/August 1994), pp. 10–14. © 1994. Reprinted with the permission of the African Publishers' Network.

Chapter 4. From *Development Dialogue* nos. 1–2 (1984), pp. 123–31. Reprinted with permission.

Chapter 5. From P. G. Altbach, ed., *Copyright and Development: Inequality in the Information Age* (1995), pp. 13-34. © 1995 Reprinted with the permission of the Bellagio Publishing Network.

Chapter 6. From the *IFLA Journal*, vol. 10, no. 4 (1984), pp. 348–56 © Reprinted with permission.

Appendix 1. From the *African Publishing Review* vol. 2, no. 5 (September/October 1993), pp. 9–11. © 1993. Reprinted with the permisson of the African Publishers' Network.

Appendix 2: From *Index on Censorship* (1996). © 1996. Reprinted with permission.

Appendix 4. From the *African Publishing Review* vol. 3, no. 5 (September/October 1994), pp. 14–15. Reprinted with the permisson of the African Publishers' Network.

Appendix 5: From the *Development Directory of Indigenous Publishing*, ed. Carol Priestley (1995). © 1995. Reprinted with the permission of the African Publishers' Network.

Foreword

CHINUA ACHEBE

Colonization is not redeemed by even its best accidental by-products, although some of them—the efflorescence of modern African literature, for example—can sometimes tease us with the possibility of such a redemption. That possibility itself is born of the special closeness between colonization and literature, between the reality of colonial subjugation and its many stories.

The colonization of Africa by Europe was built upon a body of lurid mythologies whose intent was to push Africa and Africans into a ghetto of rudimentary being outside the borders of common humanity and fellow-feeling. In response, in the fullness of time, African literary resistance emerged—beginning with the poetry of negritude in the 1930s and attaining full blossom in the fiction, poetry, and drama of the 1950s and later. It retraced its fading footprints back home from exile in a deliberate enactment of re-passage, which gave it, even when it was camouflaged in the language of exile, the inevitability and audacity of new creation myths.

One of the little side ironies attendant on colonialism was the occasional maverick who broke bounds and gained access into the ghetto in genuine solidarity. One such individual was the British publisher Alan Hill of William Heinemann. Arriving late in Africa, Hill sized up the book situation with bold originality and intelligence. He saw an enormous potential for indigenous publishing of African authors where those before him had seen only a market for British textbooks, modified, if need be, to give Jack and Jill brown faces and kinky hair. Alan Hill's success was instantaneous and huge, in service and profit. The Queen's Birthday Honours List named him Commander of the British Empire—just when there was no empire left to command, as another of Her Majesty's remarkable subjects, Alec Dickson of voluntary Service Overseas, wryly commented when he was similarly honored.

But there were, in fact, frontiers yet to conquer in the empire of the mind. Citadels of stereotype and bigotry were waiting to be dismantled with the weapon of new stories. Alan Hill had caught the vision and had the right attitude for discovering, recruiting, and inspiring a team of like-minded enthusiasts in different corners of the old empire and leaving them the initiative to get on with it. One result of his style was decisiveness. In 1962, I was attending the first ever conference of African writers at Makerere University, in Kampala, Uganda. One evening, a student called James Ngugi knocked on my door with the manuscript of his first novel, which I liked and passed on to Alan Hill's deputy, who was an observer at our conference. He immediately cabled London for direction and Hill cabled back authority to accept.

Alan Hill was of the old school of publishers who loved books and their authors and took them seriously enough to take pains and risks on their account. He liked to tell the story of a certain unprepossessing school teacher who took his first manuscript to Heinemann Publishers one Friday and received acceptance on Monday morning because old William Heinemann himself had taken the manuscript home over the weekend and read it. The teacher turned out to be D. H. Lawrence.

One of Alan Hill's star pupils was Henry Chakava, whom he snatched away from a very promising academic career in literature and philosophy and who is today one of the most pivotal indigenous publishers in Africa. His ideas, experiences, and encounters in the service and business of books are indeed worthy of our attention.

Introduction

My entry into publishing was accidental. I had just taken a First Class Honors degree in Literature and Philosophy at the University of Nairobi and had been offered a Kenya Government scholarship to pursue postgraduate studies in literature. Unfortunately, this scholarship was delayed. Bishop Stephen Neill, then professor of philosophy and religion studies at the same university, invited me to his department, offered to arrange a foreign scholarship for me, and appointed me to the position of tutorial fellow. I discussed this offer with Professor Andrew Gurr of the Literature Department and he agreed to release me, observing that there were many Kenyans undertaking postgraduate studies in English abroad. That was in May 1972.

I had a challenging stint in the Philosophy Department, teaching, learning, and undertaking research in my chosen area of African philosophy. When I finally presented my research proposal to Bishop Neill, he looked at it at length and recommended that I should enroll for the Ph.D. directly. Unfortunately, he was not able to identify a supervisor for my thesis, as he himself was not familiar with African religions, let alone African philosophy—his area of strength being comparative religion. The search for a supervisor went on for some time, and the one or two who were found recommended that I should change my thesis to some aspect of European philosophy if they were to help me. I decided to discuss my problem with Andy Gurr, who advised me to leave the Philosophy Department; he would organize a scholarship for me to the United States or United Kingdom. As I had now lost out on that academic year, he arranged for a temporary job for me in a local publishing house pending the next intake. That is how I found myself employed at the Nairobi branch office of Heinemann Educational Books Ltd. (HEB).

I joined HEB in September 1972 as a trainee editor. In addition to the general manager and the publishing manager, the company had only four other staff and occupied three rooms in downtown Nairobi. My first reaction was one of disappointment—how could a company that is so large in name be so small, and occupy such a tiny space? I consoled myself that after only six to nine months to be in this drab place I would soon be leaving for my studies. But this was not to be. Within a few weeks of my joining, the group chairman of HEB, Alan Hill, made a visit to Nairobi to meet me, and was sufficiently impressed to arrange a full training program for me, culminating in a six months' attachment at Heinemann's head office, in London. Even as I accepted all this, I had not given up on my plans to continue my postgraduate studies.

When I returned from England in December 1973, the publishing manager, David Hill, Alan Hill's son, informed me that I should prepare to take over as publishing manager by Easter 1974, as he had to return to London to take up another appointment. I was hardly two years in this job when, in April 1976, the managing director, Robert Charles Markham, had to return to England on account of his wife's bad health. So, at the tender age of thirty and with only four years experience as an editor, I was given the responsibility of managing the East African branch of HEB. At this point, and now married with a wife and a small baby, I said goodbye to my academic ambitions. In my various papers, some of which appear in this collection, I have discussed the challenges and opportunities that have come my way over these last twenty years and how I have steered East African Educational Publishers, (for this is the name Heinemann Kenya got when it went fully local four years ago), toward becoming one of the largest private enterprise publishing companies in Africa.

But back to the days of Heinemann. I believe that I have attained what I have because of the spirit that existed in Heinemann under Alan Hill. At a time when his multinational colleagues were employing Africans in their publishing houses as warehousemen, clerks, and salesmen, he hired me as an editor. He exposed me to all the training I needed to become a professional. And, above all, he entrusted me with authority and powers of decision making from the outset, and allowed me to develop my publishing lists almost unsupervised from Nairobi when other multinationals were doing it from London. I recall one editorial board meeting in London at which a secondary school English textbook for East Africa, written by the English Language Inspector in Nairobi and that I had rejected earlier came up for reconsideration. After a lengthy discussion, during which arguments for and against accepting the textbook were presented, we appeared headed for a deadlock. When Alan asked for my opinion, I said, "You cannot publish an English course for African kids based on material that is out of their cultural, social, and philosophical content. . . . If it were my decision. . . ." "But it is your decision, Henry," said Alan, and with this the course was rejected. Alan Hill's style of management is captured in his own memoir, *In Pursuit of Publishing*, and brings out the liberal but hardworking background in which I found myself, and in which I grew. My first paper on publishing was written in 1976. It was entitled "Publishing in a MultiLingual Situation: The Kenya Case," and was presented at a UNESCO conference in Alma Ata, Soviet Union, whose theme was multilingual publishing. This paper was subsequently published by Hans Zell in his journal *African Book Publishing Record*, which he had just launched. I had met Hans in Ife, Nigeria, when he organized the first conference of African book practitioners, and we struck up a friendship that has lasted to this day.

In the last twenty years, I have written more than forty papers and two monographs on publishing development in Kenya, Africa, and the developing world. These papers have dealt with all aspects of book development—from creation to production, marketing, distribution, and use. They have tackled the problems and challenges facing the publishing industry in Africa today and what needs to be done if the industry is to survive, and thrive. Wider issues such as poverty, underdevelopment, good governance, government policies, and planning, and with a focus also on education, literacy, reading, and rural transformation, have been addressed.

Several of my papers have been published as chapters in books on publishing. More than a dozen have been published and republished in academic and professional journals, newsletters, and newspapers. I have traveled extensively, especially in Africa, Europe, Asia, and North America—to conferences to present these papers, or on business, or both. I have incorporated any feedback received whenever I have revisited the same topic in another forum. Most of the essays appearing in this book were written during the ten year period between 1985 and 1995. I would have liked to rewrite some of the earlier ones, but I have left them in their original form so as to give the reader an opportunity to see how my thinking has evolved over this period.

My friend Walter Bgoya once said to me, "You cannot write so much on the same subject without repeating yourself, aren't you merely recycling yourself?" No attempt has been made to edit out repetition in these papers, if it exists. By the same token, no attempt has been made to ensure a uniform style of presentation or comprehensive coverage of all the issues at stake in African publishing. The reader might feel that there are important topics that have been left out. There is no denying that a comprehensive and systematic book dealing with all the key issues of publishing in Africa is needed, but it cannot follow the approach taken in this volume.

It is hoped that these essays, gathered in a single volume, will help to fill the gap that currently exists in the literature on this subject. The material should appeal to students of publishing development, publishing practitioners in the North and South, African governments, international donor and development agencies with book programs in the developing world, as well as the enlightened general reader. The essays do not follow a chronological or thematic pattern. For reasons already explained, there is considerable overlap, and in order to retain the spirit, atmosphere, and setting of each paper, no attempt has been made to facilitate a smooth flow of ideas. Some papers are much longer than others, and topics such as "reading" deserve a more detailed and focused attention. I am aware of these shortcomings and so is my editor, but we do not wish to interfere with the character of these papers, and the time, occasion, and audience for which they were written.

I would like to thank those who have influenced my life and career in one way or the other. In particular, I wish to single out Ngugi wa Thiong'o for inspiration and encouragement and for enlightening and emboldening my publishing vision; Professor Andrew Gurr for nurturing and shaping my life's direction; David Hill, R. C. Markham, Aig Higo, Hans Zell, James Currey, Keith Sambrook, Sven Hamrell, Per Gedin, and Olle Nordberg, for their long professional association; Walter Bgoya for sharp, critical, and resilient friendship; and Philip Altbach for suggesting that I consider publishing these essays in book form. Finally, I would like to thank my friend Jonas Sademaki of Governors Camp, Maasai Mara, for providing facilities for the writing of some of these papers, all my staff and colleagues at EAEP for making it such a nice place to work, and my wife Roselyn and children Sharon, Laura, and Yolanda for their understanding and patient endurance of my frequent absences from home.

February 1996

1

Kenyan Publishing: Independence and Dependence

Very little has been written on the Kenyan publishing industry even though it is one of the most important in Africa. The aim of this chapter is to attempt, for the first time, to discuss the origins and development, the successes and failures, the opportunities and challenges of the Kenyan book industry as comprehensively as possible, from the time of Kenya's independence to the present day.

AT INDEPENDENCE

At the time of independence, there were only three major publishers on the scene. The first, East African Literature Bureau (EALB), had been started by the East African High Commission (the common services organ of the British colonial government of Kenya, Uganda and Tanzania) in 1948 in response to demand from the emerging African readership for relevant homegrown reading materials following recommendations by the Elspeth Education Commission. Charles Richards, an experienced missionary printer-cum-publisher was appointed to run it.

In fact, Richards was largely responsible for the arrival of the other two publishers, Longman and Oxford University Press. He has argued consistently that it was his wish right from the beginning to support the growth of a vibrant local publishing industry in Kenya.[1] For example, instead of installing printing facilities at EALB, he encouraged commercial printers to print for him. On the publishing side, he invited British publishers to open branches in Kenya, offering to pass over to them for exploitation any viable titles developed at the Bureau.

From P. G. Altbach, ed., *Publishing and Development in the Third World*, 1992 pp. 119–50.

The Coming of Foreign Publishers

Longman, which was already publishing for the market—but from London, was the first to respond, appointing a resident representative in 1950. Oxford University Press arrived four years later and set up an office very much along the lines followed by Longman. Neither company published locally; rather their function was to collect good manuscripts and forward them to London for vetting and publishing. Richards became a regular supplier of EALB-developed books to these companies, and they managed through this arrangement to publish some very profitable textbooks such as Oxford's *New Oxford English Course for East Africa* and Longman's *Highway Arithmetic*. Local printing did not start until 1965, two years after independence.

We shall mention three other categories of publishers who were active at this time although they are not central to our present study. These were the Government Printer, whose work from its initiation in 1899 was the printing of government notices, reports, and so on; it is still functioning today, but it never ventured into mainstream publishing. Among the others are the mission presses—spearheaded by the Church Missionary Society, which is reported to have printed the first Kenyan book in 1894, thereby setting in motion and eventually helping to shape the emergence of a local publishing industry. The prime concern of the mission presses was the translation of the Bible and the hymn book into African languages and any other books that they considered important for the spiritual nourishment of their newly converted followers. And after World War II, there were also small presses operated by Kenyan nationalists such as Henry Muoria and, later, Gakaara wa Wanjau, who produced handbills, political pamphlets, and booklets in their efforts to sensitize the African people in the early stages of the freedom movement, and for an alternative education from that offered by the missionaries.

Richards' About-Turn

As can be seen, there was neither a privately owned local publishing house, nor a national one, at the time of independence. It is important to appreciate this point if one wants to understand the things that hampered and, in a way, still hamper the development of a strong indigenous publishing industry in Kenya. One person best placed to spearhead its establishment at the time of independence was none other than Charles Richards himself He had done a good job publishing for the Church Missionary Society in the 1930s, had been instrumental in the establishment of Ndia Kuu Press (the first Kenyan commercial publisher) in the 1940s, and had managed EALB from its inception to 1963, when he resigned to become the manager of the newly locally incorporated branch of Oxford University Press. For some time, he continued to enjoy a special relationship with EALB, out of which the profitable and perennial *New Peak English Course* arose.

We must state at the outset that we do not believe in state publishing and are suspicious of the efficacy of parastatal organizations. We are, therefore, in full sympathy with Richards when he justifies his decision to invite commercial publishers and to launch them off with ready-made textbooks from EALB. But we should have thought that if Richards believed in commercial publishing, he would have crowned his exemplary service to publishing in Kenya by spearheading, at independence, the establishment of a locally owned commercial firm. Such a firm would have benefited from his policy of shedding off successful textbooks to enable the bureau to concentrate on his prescribed noble task of developing materials for the new literates. J. W. Chege has questioned the reasoning behind Richards' policy of developing texts and then handing them over to foreign publishers. He argues, and with the benefit of hindsight quite rightly so, that by doing this the bureau was preparing the ground for the entrenchment of foreign publishers, particularly Longman, Oxford University Press, Macmillan, and Nelson. He goes on,

> This meant that the Bureau bore all the publishing risks for these commercial publishers. . . . They did not have to spend their money on marketing research, or sales promotion. . . . The risks were borne by the Bureau which could only afford to do this at the expense of the East African tax-payer.[2]

However well intentioned Charles Richards may have been, he lost a major opportunity to leave a national monument behind after 30 years of credible service to Kenya, unleashing instead a multinational ogre that was to dominate the postindependence publishing scene for many years.

CREATING NEW INSTITUTIONS

The period after independence was one of change, experimentation, and innovation. Education, acknowledged as the key to national development, was one of the first areas to receive attention. The Kenya Institute of Education (KIE) was set up in 1964, amalgamated with the Curriculum Development Center and charged with the responsibility of drawing up new syllabi reflecting the changed priorities of the newly independent state. The first Commission of Enquiry into education, under the chairmanship of Professor S. H. Ominde, was appointed to undertake an exhaustive inquiry into all aspects of education in Kenya. The commission submitted part one of its report in October 1964, with wide-ranging recommendations that were to have far-reaching effects on the direction of education in Kenya. Although books are critical to the success of any education system, the report said nothing about them and how they were to be created, produced and distributed to serve the educational system the committee had so meticulously analyzed and restructured. And because no mention was made of books in this very vital report, about which more will be said later, a major opportunity to propose a national book publishing and distribution policy was lost.

However, the syllabi being developed by KIE and the materials that were produced by the subsequent subject panels underscored the need to have a publisher who would issue these materials. So the government created Jomo Kenyatta Foundation (JKF) in 1965 as a trust that would publish these materials and use whatever profits it made in the award of scholarships to needy children. It must be emphasized that although government later got sensitive about primary school books being published by foreign commercial publishers, and later unsuccessfully tried to use JKF as a primary school publisher, the problem was that JKF had not been set up as part of a broad national strategy toward localizing the Kenyan book industry.

THE COMING OF LOCAL PUBLISHERS

1965 was a watershed year for Kenyan publishing. Apart from JKF, several other new publishers came on the scene—the most important of which was, perhaps, East African Publishing House (EAPH). It was started by a group of academics from Eastern Africa who constituted the East African Institute of Social and Cultural Affairs, in association with the British publisher Andre Deutsch. The new publisher was expected to cater more satisfactorily to the academic and general educational needs of the local communities and to reflect a more positive image of the African heritage, which, it was felt, the existing foreign publishers had failed to do. The partnership with Andre Deutsch did not last and was discontinued the following year due to differences arising from publishing policies. Institute members then formed themselves into the East African Cultural Trust, which was to administer the publishing house, and Afropress, a sister printing works established later. The new firm was able to attract manuscripts especially from academics who were themselves members of the institute, with quite a few of their own titles coming out during the firm's first few years of publishing.

Another new publishing company that started business in 1965 was Equatorial Publishers, a private indigenous publisher set up by an entrepreneuring ex-salesman of Longman named Y. N. Okal, who also spread his interests to include bookshops and a printing press.

In the same year two foreign publishers, Longman and Heinemann, set up substantive branches. Longman, who by now had two very successful textbooks, the *Highway Arithmetic* and *Pivot English Course*, consolidated its gains by reconstituting itself into an overseas branch of Longman U.K., and in 1969 as a full company, Longman Kenya Ltd. As for Heinemann, it at first thought that its general list might appeal to the ex-colonial settlers who admittedly made up much of the general readership, and a new company, Heinemann-Cassell, was formed to carry the trade list. Heinemann soon afterwards found out that the African Writers Series and key textbooks such as *Ordinary Level Physics* and *New Certificate Chemistry* stood it in good stead. Three years later, the general company was dissolved and a new educational company, Heinemann Educational Books (E.A.) Ltd., was established in 1968. Macmillan came seeking to employ the same strategy as it had done in Ghana, Tanzania, and Uganda, but it did not find a willing state publisher to work with and had to wait until 1971, when it registered itself locally as (Macmillan) Books for Africa after its debacle in the three countries above had necessitated a fresh start.

Other publishers such as Nelson, Evans, Pitman, and Cambridge University Press, to name a few, were active at this time and appointed resident representatives. A host of other British publishers who neither had branches nor representatives in Kenya offered agencies to those who were already there, so that by about 1968, close to 80 British publishers had some form of presence in Kenya. So, during the first five years of Kenya's independence, there were, apart from the Government Printer and the religious presses, four types of publishers coexisting amicably but potentially antagonistically with one another: the state or semistate publishers (for example, EAPH), private commercial publishers (Equatorial), and foreign publishers (Longman, Oxford University Press, Heinemann). At first, there were no major problems between the main groups or within each group; in fact, there seems to have been some cooperation. For example, Oxford University Press continued to publish the *New Peak English Course*, originally developed by EALB, refined by KIE, and now renamed *Progressive Peak English Course*. Longman copublished the title *Zamani: A Survey of East African History*, edited by B. A. Ogot, with EAPH. And, again, Longman was the publisher chosen to produce *Tujifunze Kusoma Kikwetu*—an ambitious language and reading scheme developed at KIE, in which the same color illustrations were to be used to produce the textbook in 15 local-language editions. The EAPH developed a mathematics course, *School Mathematics of East Africa (SMEA)* jointly with Cambridge University Press.

By 1970 it could be said that although Kenya had been independent for seven years, the publishing industry was largely in the hands of foreign publishers. Equatorial publishers were finding the going difficult and were surviving mostly on what they made from their printing press. The JKF was deriving most of its revenue from *Kenya Primary Mathematics*, a complete primary mathematics textbook developed at KIE, and a few teachers' guides. EAPH, either by choice or force of circumstances, was publishing mainly academic and general books, children's books and fiction, while the EALB continued on the path that Richards had charted for it on his departure, namely publishing books in African languages and adult literacy primers. The profitable textbook market, which at that time represented over 80 percent of the value of the total book market, was in the hands of foreign publishers. John Nottingham, then executive director of EAPH, has covered this period well in his various papers, drawing attention to this acute dependence in a sensitive area of vital national interest.[3]

The first response to this multinational stranglehold came from government. They set up the Kenya School Equipment Scheme (KSES), a body that was to buy books centrally and distribute them to Kenya's primary schools. The Ministry of Education then proceeded to draw up a list of recommended books to be bought by the KSES, and this included titles mainly developed at KIE and published by the JKF. As the foundation had not yet published all the books required for primary schools, the ministry had no alternative but to include textbooks from foreign publishers as well. But the government intended to protect the primary school market as a monopoly for JKF. In fact, so successful was KSES, that titles outside the scheme's list sold in very small quantities indeed—the losers being largely foreign publishers of primary school books, with textbooks such as JKF's *Safari English Course* gaining ground on the more acceptable traditional books.

The second response came from local entrepreneurs entering the publishing business—among them John Nottingham, who had resigned from East African Publishing House to set up Transafrica Publishers and Book Distributors in 1973. Fred Ojienda, the production man at EAPH, also broke off to set up Foundation Books in 1974. Others were David Maillu, a graphic artist and illustrator, who established Comb Books in 1972 with the main intention of publishing his own novels—to which local publishers had not reacted favorably. Other publishers coming on the scene included Njogu Gitene—Njogu Gitene Publications (children's books); Lennard Okola—Bookwise (educational); Ngotho Kariuki—Midi Teki (general); Abdilahi Nassir—Shungwaya (Kiswahili general); Mohammed Mbwana—Mowa (Kiswahili educational); and Munuhe Kareithi—Gazelle Books (educational/general).

THE FAT YEARS

The period between 1970 and 1977 was probably the most lively in Kenyan publishing, and the most competitive. The JKF monopoly described above did not work completely, as the foundation did not have all the primary schoolbooks required in the system. So with the exception of *Kenya Primary Mathematics*, a Kiswahili textbook entitled *Masomo Ya Kiswahili*, and the *Safari Course*, KSES procured the rest of the required materials from commercial publishers, the majority of which were still branches of multinational publishers. The indigenous publishers did not have the kind of funding required to develop textbooks that would have gotten onto the scheme, but they did get several single titles onto it. Although there was general prosperity, this period was characterized by doubt, mutual suspicion, and intrigue among the parties involved. Paradoxically, it is this situation that led to the formation of important professional associations in 1971—the Kenya Publishers Association and the Kenya African Booksellers and Stationers Association, later named the Kenya Booksellers and Stationers Association, so as to accommodate all the nationalities involved in the book trade. It would appear that people joined these associations to guard their own self-interests rather than to strive for the common goal of working toward the welfare of the book industry as a whole. It comes as no surprise that five years later, indigenous publishers had pulled out of the Kenya Publishers Association, while the Kenya African Booksellers Association was finding it difficult to continue without the support of its more affluent Asian partners.

The Lean Years

The period of prosperity ended in 1977, with the closure of the border between Kenya and Tanzania. Kenyan publishers were no longer able to export to Tanzania or the markets farther south such as Zambia and Malawi. There had been little business with Uganda since Idi Amin's 1971 coup d'état. Thus, over this period Kenyans had lost the bulk of their export trade, which at its peak had averaged 25 to 30 percent of their turnover. To complicate matters, the home market stagnated largely as a result of the uncertainty surrounding Daniel arap Moi's succession to the presidency upon Kenyatta's death in 1978. A coup attempt on President Moi's new government in 1982 did not help matters.

The response to these problems was varied. Longman, by far the largest publisher, reacted by selling 40 percent of its equity to local people—more as a way of ensuring their own survival than as a genuine step toward indigenizing the company. And when this approach seemed not to be working, they followed the example set by Oxford University Press in declaring some staff redundant and cutting down on their publishing programs. The smaller foreign publishers (e.g., Collins, Pitmans, Cambridge University Press, Nelsons, and Evans), either closed down completely or pulled out and left their businesses in the hands of local commission agents.

State-supported publishers such as EAPH, Kenya Literature Bureau (KLB), the company that Kenya had set up in 1979 to replace the former EALB, and the JKF were all dormant, with almost no new titles coming out of them during this critical period.

But it was the indigenous publishers who took the greatest beating. Transafrica went bankrupt, while Comb Books, Foundation Books, Shungwaya, Mowa, Midi Teki, Bookwise, Njogu Gitene, all stopped publishing and, with no backlists to fall back on, went out of business. EAPH was eventually declared bankrupt in 1987.

The Advent of the 8-4-4 Education System

The announcement of the new 8-4-4 education system came as a shot in the arm for Kenyan publishing. The government had appointed a Presidential Working Party in 1981 under the chairmanship of Professor C. B. Mackay, to look into the feasibility of establishing a second university for Kenya. In going about this assignment, the commission reviewed the whole structure of education in Kenya and was guided in this exercise by the Gachathi Report on Educational Objectives and Policies. The principal aim was to come up with an education system that equipped children with enough practical skills to make them self-reliant after primary school. The Gachathi Report's recommendation that they should stay in primary school for nine years as opposed to the then seven was found to be too expensive to implement. Mackay came forward with a compromise of eight years in primary school, and a new Kenyan education system was born. "A" levels were abolished, the number of years spent at university was increased to a minimum of four years. Thus the new system provided for eight years at primary school, four years at secondary, and at least four years at university (8-4-4). To achieve its other aim, the committee increased the number of subjects to be examined in Standard Eight from 3 (English, mathematics, general paper), to 11, (English, mathematics, Kiswahili, science, geography-history-civics, religious education (Islamic or Christian), music, home science, agriculture, arts and crafts and business education). Funding was obtained from the World Bank to facilitate speedy development of the syllabi and teaching materials, and the new system was launched in January 1985, catching everyone unaware, including all publishers. Even more challenging was the fact that it was initiated at the Standard Eight level, and the need to develop new books for this class and all the others before and after it was urgent.

Books for the 8-4-4 Educational System

At first, it was a free-for-all, and money was made particularly by the new or existing do-it-yourself publishers, who were able to get their books onto the market faster than were the established publishers. One such person to benefit, in that climate, was Johnstone Makau, whose new company, Kenya Publishing and Book Marketing Co. Ltd., was the most promising indigenous publishing venture Kenyans had seen for some time. Another was Gideon S. Were, whose press of the same name was started at around this time but not necessarily with the view to cashing in on the 8-4-4 windfall. When textbooks from the established publishers arrived later, they were found to be better, and many schools switched textbooks in midstream. The resulting wastage caused an uproar and much confusion, particularly since in some cases there were three or four textbooks in use in any one school. Parents sought guidance from the Ministry of Education not only about the content but also the prices of these publications.

Response from the ministry was swift. Subject panels were set up to prepare official textbooks for all the subjects in primary and secondary schools and these were published by the two state publishers—JKF and KLB. Apparently funds to facilitate this process were provided by the World Bank. When the books appeared, schools were informed that these were the only recommended textbooks and that no other textbooks should be used. As the KSES had already been disbanded, it was not possible for the ministry to control the purchasing of these publications, but directives were sent out to head teachers and education officers to ensure that only government textbooks were bought. This seems to have been effective, for within a few months, sales of competing textbooks from commercial houses had dropped considerably.

Unfortunately, although the government textbooks are generally about 20 percent cheaper than those of commercial publishers, they have been criticized as being amateurish in layout and illustrations, shallow and unbalanced in their content—problems that doubtlessly arise from their multiple authorship and the speed with which they were written and produced. The ministry has been warned about the dangers inherent in the incestuous process of writing, vetting, publishing, and buying its own books, as this can neither serve the interests of publishing nor of education at large. Once again, the private commercial publisher in Kenya is under siege unless the recently announced review of the 8-4-4 education system lifts the monopoly currently enjoyed by state publishing parastatal firms.

THE PRESENT: STATE OF THE ART

Compared to other countries in East and Central Africa, Kenya has the most active book industry. In part one of this study, we traced the historical development of this industry from independence to the present, while highlighting the principal actors involved. In this section, we shall examine the industry itself, from a structural and quantitative point of view, in order to determine what kind of literature is being produced and in what numbers.

My UNESCO monograph gives a detailed analysis and statistical data on the sound infrastructure that supports Kenyan publishing.[4] Although this information is now somewhat dated, it is generally still valid as nothing has happened in the intervening period to displace or disrupt it. The country still has adequate printing capacity, with more than 10 printers capable of achieving a reasonably good standard of book production. The Panafrican Paper Mill at Webuye, in western Kenya, continues to produce adequate paper to meet the country's needs, having recently increased its capacity from 65,000 to 100,000 tons per annum. Foreign exchange is available for the importation of plates, films, boards, stitches, and other types of paper and book-production inputs essential for book production but not available locally.

The market has expanded quite considerably. In 1980 the country's population was estimated to be about 16 million, compared to current estimates of about 22 million. The number of school-going children has increased from the figure of 4 million in my monograph to 5,123,581 in 1988. The number of bookshops has doubled from the figure of 205 in my 1980 report to 400, largely as a result of the abolition of the KSES in 1984 and the introduction of the 8-4-4 education system in 1985. So, generally, the infrastructure has expanded in favor of Kenyan publishing during the last few years, and this is clearly demonstrated in Table 1, which shows a dramatic increase in the number of new books published in the years between 1985 and 1989. It should be noted that the number of new titles may be larger than the figures contained in this table—as contrary to regulations, state publishers appear not to be registering their new publications with the Registrar of Books, the source of our information.

A breakdown of these publications according to Universal Decimal Classification is presented in Table 2. As can be seen, quite a large number of the titles were religious publications from a number of mission presses, which have a long tradition of activity in the market. Their role will be discussed briefly later, as we consider them to be largely outside the scope of the present study. The new titles under "Languages" appear numerous because all publications in African languages have been grouped in this category.

Table 1
New Books and Pamphlets: 1985–1989

Year	Books	Pamphlets	Total
1985	109	6	115
1986	141	12	153
1987	174	20	194
1988	167	57	224
1989	294	65	359

Table 2
New Titles According to Universal Decimal Classification

	1985	1986	1987	1988	1989
General	10	11	10	22	24
Philosophy	2	—	3	2	3
Religion	36	65	27	38	104
Social Sciences	5	3	7	11	14
Pure Sciences	7	12	36	19	33
Applied Sciences (technical)	7	10	21	30	37
Arts	6	6	8	9	22
Languages	26	19	39	22	53
Literature	9	15	16	56	32
General History and Geography	7	12	27	15	37
Total	115	153	194	224	359

Having now shown the subject spread, we shall proceed with a thematic analysis of the industry's output to see what kind of picture emerges.

Textbooks

Textbooks are, without a doubt, the bread and butter of the Kenyan publishing industry. It has been estimated that 90 percent of Kenya's book business is derived from textbooks. In fact, it can be said that the reason why Kenya's indigenous publishers have failed is because they have been unable to break into the lucrative textbook market. The reasons for this are easy to appreciate. Textbooks take time and money to develop. They require experienced authors, editors, text designers, illustrators, and a host of ancillary personnel to see them through production. And when the books get printed, a massive promotional and advertising campaign requiring more money and a large force of salespeople follows. If the campaign is successful and the textbook is adopted, the publisher is assured of a steady seller for many years to come. The leading publishers in Kenya today have at least one textbook that serves as the backbone of their business—for example, JKF's *Primary Mathematics,* Oxford Press's *New Peak English Course,* Heinemann's *Masomo Ya Msingi,* and Longman's *Msingi Wa Kiswahili.* A publisher must always be aware of the risks involved, of the danger that its textbook might not secure adoption. A publisher who has already succeeded with one text is in a better position to risk investing in another one. The textbook market is a struggle of the fittest, and the indigenous publisher, already financially disadvantaged, is also historically disadvantaged, having come on the scene after the foreign branches had already entrenched themselves.

The number of textbooks published during the five years between 1985 and 1989 as a percentage of all books published is shown in Table 3. As can be seen, textbooks comprised, on average, 54 percent of all the books published. In reality, this percentage is higher for the reason mentioned earlier—namely, that state publishers JKF and KLB, who exclusively publish textbooks, appear not to have registered their new titles with the Registrar of Books during the period under review.

We have already discussed moves by the government to secure a monopoly in the publishing of textbooks for primary and secondary schools and must now point out the consequences of such a move should it succeed. It is inconceivable that a commercial publisher can succeed in the Kenyan market without having a share of the textbook market. In fact, those publishers who have been able to publish in the areas of fiction, adult literacy, children's books, and general and academic books have done this using money made from textbook publishing. As the government tightens its grip on the textbook market, commercial publishers will respond by suspending any nonviable or risky ventures and will at first concentrate on developing supplementary, adapted, and other textbooks for schools. If things do not improve, redundancies and even bankruptcies will follow, just as occurred during the late 1970s and early 1980s. And more publishers may be involved this time: Longman and Heinemann, now being local majority-owned companies, will not be bailed out by their parent companies as before. Commercial publishing will gradually die, and the book industry will slowly disappear, giving way to state parastatals, which will once more resort to the KSES-type of book-distribution network as before. This is what happened in Tanzania, Zambia, and Uganda toward the end of the 1960s. By the mid-1970s, there were no books in those countries—not even from the parastatals that had been given the monopoly to serve those markets in preference to commercial publishers. Commercial publishers who might have been called upon to salvage the situation had long vacated the scene, or gone into some other business.

Table 3
Percentage of Textbooks Published

Year Published	Total Number of Books	Number of Textbooks	% of Textbooks
1985	115	55	47.8
1986	153	67	43.8
1987	194	139	71.6
1988	224	122	54.5
1989	359	191	53.5

Source: Registrar of Books, Department of the Registrar-General, Office of the Attorney-General, Nairobi

Kenya would be well advised to discontinue state monopoly in publishing and to free the industry to market forces. After all, the circumstances that existed when the monopoly was announced no longer apply. The bad books have been pushed out, and now there is a wide range of good textbooks on the market, in some subjects as many as four. Schools now have a wide range of options to choose from. Longman and Heinemann, the two largest commercial publishers, have in the meantime come under the control of the Kenyan nationals; so it is no longer a question of rescuing the industry from the jaws of foreign multinational publishers, as has been so consistently stated in the past.

RELIGIOUS BOOKS

Religious books constitute the second-largest category of books published in Kenya. The books are issued mostly by mission presses, which have been active in the country since the turn of the century and which, as we saw earlier, were responsible for bringing printing and publishing into the country. Their publications, which remain largely the same as when they started, consist mainly of translations of the Bible, the hymn book, and other liturgy and Bible stories from English into Kiswahili and other local languages. The books are cheaply priced, no doubt as a result of subsidies from the mother churches. They are then distributed throughout the country, by means of church networks that include bona fide church bookshops in key towns.

Evangel Publishing House, Bible Society of Kenya, Uzima Press, St. Paul's Publications, African Inland Church, Daystar, and Baptist Publishing House are some of the most active of these publishers. A common feature with all of them is that they print, publish, and distribute their own books—the latter so efficiently that commercial publishers may have something to learn from them. The number of religious publications in relation to textbooks and the total number of books published is shown in Table 4. This means that, on average, nearly 80 percent of the books published over the last five years have been either textbooks or religious books, leaving the remaining subject areas with only 20 percent. This point underscores the importance of textbooks to the industry since, it can be argued, religious books fall outside the scope of the commercial publishing sector largely on account of the different ways in which churches create, price, and distribute their publications.

Table 4
Textbooks and Religious Books as a Percentage of all Books Published (Number of Titles)

	1985	1986	1987	1988	1989
Total Books Published	115	153	194	224	359
Number of Textbooks	55	67	139	122	191
% Textbooks	41.8	43.8	71.6	54.5	53.2
Religious Books	34	62	21	37	88
% Religious Books	29.6	40.5	10.8	16.5	24.5
Textbooks and Religious Books as % of all books published	77.4	84.3	82.4	71.0	77.7

FICTION

Under this category, we shall cover creative writings of all genres, including novels, poetry, drama, popular fiction, and oral literature. Fiction has a relatively short history in Kenya, dating back to 1964 when Heinemann published *Weep Not Child*, a novel by Kenya's foremost novelist, Ngugi wa Thiong'o, currently living in exile. This was immediately followed by *The River Between* (1965) and *A Grain of Wheat* (1967). It was the success that Ngugi's writings were having that partly convinced Heinemann to set up a local office in Nairobi in 1965. After this time, titles from their African Writers Series were regularly prescribed for study by the East African Examination Council, which was established in 1967.

The ambition to appear in the African Writers Series was great among local writers, and the local office was kept busy receiving, processing, and forwarding promising manuscripts to London for consideration and possible publication. Some of the authors whose works were published arising from this arrangement were Taban lo Liyong, Meja Mwangi, Mwangi Ruheni, Okot p'Bitek, and Joe de Graft—to name but a few.

This beginning led to a flowering of all sorts of literature in the early 1970s, with the newly established local publishers making a major contribution. EAPH, in particular, launched its Modern African Library, in which exciting trail-blazing works such as Okot p'Bitek's *Song of Lawino* and *Song of Ocol* and Charles Mangua's *Son of Woman* were published. Their Poets of Africa Series included explosive works like

Margaret Dickenson's *When Bullets Begin to Flower*, a collection of poetry by Angolan freedom fighters, and many more. Longman launched its Drumbeat Series in which they published local creative writers. Oxford University Press set up its New Drama from Africa and New Fiction from Africa Series, in which perhaps the most important find was John Ruganda, Uganda's leading playwright.

Local publishers, led by David Maillu with his Comb Books, also played a role, particularly in the proliferation of popular fiction in the mid-1970s. Maillu's titles such as *After 4:30, My Dear Bottle, Unfit for Human Consumption, Diary of a Prostitute* took the market by storm and sold in the thousands. Other publishers jumped on the bandwagon with similar entertainment reading materials, though slightly highbrow and less lurid than Maillu's. Heinemann launched Spear Books, Longman started Longman Crime Series, and Transafrica had Afromances. Some of the successful books that came out of this were Hillary Ngweno's *The Men from Pretoria* (Longman) and John Kariamiti's *My Life in Crime* (Spear). The closure of the common border between Kenya and Tanzania, compounded with the problems that faced the industry between 1977 and 1984, effectively put a stop to this kind of publishing—with most of the publishers going out of business.

Currently there is not much publishing activity in fiction, partly because of the uncertainty surrounding the future of commercial publishing in the country and the rush to fill up any gaps that might still remain in the 8-4-4 education syllabus. Over the last five years, only an average of 25 titles have been published per year, representing 12 percent of the total number of titles published over the period. Quite a number of titles published in 1988 and 1989 are in fact guides to prescribed texts studied at school, and while they qualify as works of literary criticism, they belong more to the category of textbooks rather than to fiction.

Although a few titles still come out of Longman, the market leader is, without a doubt, Heinemann Kenya. It has published nearly 30 key novels under license from the African Writers Series published by its parent company in the United Kingdom. Heinemann Kenya has issued a number of local titles of its own, including Marjorie Oludhe Macgoye's prize-winning historical novel, *Coming to Birth*. And when EAPH went bankrupt, Heinemann Kenya moved in to rescue a number of key titles, among them Okot p'Bitek's *Song of Lawino* and *Ocol*, Francis Imbuga's *Betrayal in the City*, Charles Mangua's *Son of Woman*, Grace Ogot's *Land without Thunder*, Margaret Dickinson's *When Bullets*

Begin to Flower, and all of John Ruganda's plays. Heinemann Kenya continues to publish at least four new titles annually in the Spears Series, a popular paperback imprint launched in the mid-1970s and now with nearly 30 titles in print. But, on the whole, there is a paucity of local reading materials, and most of what is read is still imported.

ORAL LITERATURE

Oral Literature is the other genre that came into existence in the 1970s. It was the culmination of a debate in the English Department of the University of Nairobi. Ngugi wa Thiong'o, with the support of his African colleagues, had successfully advocated the abolition of the English Department and its replacement by a Literature Department, in which the study of African literature would be at the center. The importance of oral literature in this new scenario was recognized at once, and moves were made to popularize it nationwide. At a historic meeting of secondary school teachers of literature in Nairobi in 1974, it was unanimously agreed that oral literature be introduced in all Kenyan secondary schools. As a result, Heinemann Kenya issued the first textbook in this subject, *Oral Literature: A School Certificate Course*, and launched a series of ethnic studies. *Oral Literature of the Maasai, Oral Literature of the Gikuyu*, and *Oral Literature of the Kalenjin* have already appeared, while others are still under preparation. Indeed, oral literature as a subject for study in schools has attracted considerable interest among local publishers.

CHILDREN'S BOOKS

This area is probably the most underdeveloped in Kenyan publishing in spite of its potential. This is so for several reasons. Until recently, nursery schools were not part of the formal education system in Kenya and no standardized syllabi for preprimary education existed. Children got into primary school without being exposed to any reading materials. There were no libraries in primary schools, and no provision was made for reading on school timetables. Most children came from homes with illiterate parents and no reading facilities. At the end of the day, all the textbooks were turned in, to be handed back the following morning.

Kenyan children started getting exposed to nontextbook reading materials at independence, when schools were desegregated and some Africans were allowed to go to schools formerly reserved for whites. Here, they were given colorful imported books that transported them to strange places, among people whose lifestyles did not bear the slightest resemblance to their own. Unknowingly, the country found itself producing a new breed of black Europeans, who began to despise their own skin and background. This process, which started at independence, is still going on today. Reading lists from most primary schools in Nairobi still contain such titles as *Famous Five Stories*, the Nancy Drew Series, *Janet and John*, the *Hardy Boys*, *Topsy and Tim*, and *Reading 360*.

EAPH was the first to attempt to break the monopoly enjoyed by foreign children's books in the Kenyan market. It launched its Lioncub series, and by 1976, it had published 10 books—among them Chinua Achebe's *How the Leopard Got His Claws*. EAPH's East African *When, Why and How* series by Pamela Kola, also published around this time, was favorably received by the market. Longman's Reading Scheme, with such titles as *Hare is Here, Hare is Bad*, made some impact. But between 1978 and 1986, very few new children's books were published. Apart from being slow sellers, children's books are difficult and expensive to produce as one has to use tough paper, employ full-color illustrations, and bind in boards. And there is also the problem of deciding what language to write them in since most Kenyan children between the ages of 6 and 10 are simultaneously introduced to English and Kiswahili, along with their mother tongue.

There is, at the moment, renewed interest in children's books in Kenya. Heinemann has recently launched two children's book series, Elementary Readers and Junior Readers and has recently brought into the country authors Chinua Achebe (1988) and Cyprian Ekwensi (1990) to help launch and promote writing for children in Kenya. A new company, Phoenix, rising from the ashes of the defunct EAPH, has reissued some of its children's books under Phoenix Young Readers Library and is now following up with some original works. Asenath Odaga's Lake Publishers, based in Kenya's lake town of Kisumu, in Western Kenya, is also experimenting with children's books in English and the mother tongue. All these publishers have had to refashion their own concept of a children's book to adjust to the financial realities of the Kenyan market. A lot of the books they are issuing now are printed on ordinary 70gsm printing paper, illustrated in one or two colors, and bound softback with saddle stitches. Consequently, prices are affordable and sales are reported to be generally improving. Finally, two new associations, the Children's Literature Association of Kenya and the Council for the Promotion of Science Publications for Children in Africa, have been formed, with a view to promoting children's books in Kenya and Africa as a whole. The country may have to rely on imported children's books for some time to come since Kenyan publishers are still faced with many obstacles before they are able to assert themselves fully and competitively in this tricky market.

ADULT LITERACY

Just like the children's books discussed above, the language factor plays a role in the publication of adult literacy materials. When the EALB started in 1948, its principle assignment was "to publish books for Africans both for general reading and educational purposes, in English and African languages." So great was the demand for these books that Charles Richards was able to report in June 1956 that over 350 titles, with a total of 1.75 million volumes, had been printed, out of which 50 titles, with a total of 330,000 volumes, had been reprinted.[5] It is likely that these numbers had doubled by the time Richards left EALB in 1963. As pointed out earlier, the bureau continued to publish in this area up to 1977, when it folded up following the collapse of the East African Community.

All these materials were written in Kiswahili and more than 15 other Kenyan languages. Most of the books were rather thin, consisting mostly of real or imagined stories, cultural information and how-to functional readers. Sadly, the KLB did not take on the responsibility of keeping these books in print when it succeeded EALB in 1979.

Some of the materials that we discussed as religious books are of an adult literacy nature and contain guidelines on how to be clean in body and soul, and hints on matters of agriculture, family life, and so on. But the responsibility for initiating adult literacy materials lies squarely with the Board of Adult Education in the Ministry of Culture and Social Services. Unfortunately, the board suffers from a shortage of teachers and relevant books. It has developed some materials and could benefit from the services of a publisher, to get them published, but the board seems to want to do its own publishing. In spite of the very high hopes that the board would spearhead the nation toward eradication of adult illiteracy by 1983, only one million people had been rescued by then; these people are reported to be in danger of lapsing back into illiteracy if reading materials for continuing education are not made available to them. This is an area to which the revitalized state publishing firms must turn if the new dream of universal literacy by the year 2000 is to be achieved.

GENERAL BOOKS

Most of the general books written about Kenya have been published outside the country. These consist largely of nostalgic and euphoric memoirs by or biographies and autobiographies of ex-colonial settlers and administrators. These books appear to be very popular among tourists and have formed some kind of colonial subculture in independent Kenya. Examples include Karen Blixen's *Out of Africa*, which was reprinted no less than six times when a film of the same title was released in 1986, and Elspeth Huxley's *The Flame Trees of Thika*, which was reprinted four times in 1981 when a film based on the same book was released. Other examples include *The Happy Valley* (1979) by Michael Best, *White Mischief* (1982) by James Fox, *Silence Will Speak* (1977) and *The Kenya Pioneers* (1980) by Errol Trizebinki, *So Rough a Wind* (1964) by Michael Blundell, *Evelyn Baring—The Last Proconsul* (1978) by Douglas Huma, *My Pride and Joy* (1986) by George Adamson, *West with the Night* (1984) by Beryl Markham, *The Legendary Grogan* (1981) by L. Farrant, and so on: the list is long.

On the other hand, response from the Kenyan freedom fighters has been half-hearted at best and muted at worst. There is only Jomo Kenyatta's *Suffering without Bitterness* (1968), J. M. Kariuki's *"Mau Mau" Detainee* (1965), Bildad Kaggia's *Roots of Freedom* (1975), Waruhiu Itote's *Mau Mau General* (1967), Muthoni Likimani's *Passbook Number F47927* (1985), and Gakaara wa Wanjau's *Mwandiki wa Mau Mau Ithamirio-ini* (1983)—translated as *Mau Mau Author in Detention* (1988)—winner of the 1984 Noma Award for Publishing in Africa. Their other books of general and academic interest include Jomo Kenyatta's *Facing Mount Kenya* (1938), Oginga Odinga's *Not Yet Uhuru* (1967), Tom Mboya's *Freedom and After* (1963) and *The Challenge of Nationhood* (1975), Ngugi wa Thiong'o's *Detained: A Writer's Prison Diary* (1980), and President Daniel arap Moi's *Kenya African Nationalism* (1987).

There is no doubt that a market exists for general books in Kenya. The Kenyan publisher must stop dabbling solely in textbooks and spread out into areas vital to the life and culture of the nation. Oxford University Press and Heinemann, the two publishers who have done some publishing in this area, have pointed out that Kenya's leaders appear to be hesitant to come forward to tell their own stories.

ACADEMIC AND TECHNICAL BOOKS

Here we shall deal with publishing for all postsecondary educational institutions such as universities, polytechnics, medical and teacher training colleges, and professional schools. The majority of the books used at these institutions are still largely imported, mostly from Britain and India. In the past, it has been considered nonviable to publish for this market because it was so small. But it is now estimated that Kenya's four public universities will have a total enrollment of over 40,000; technical colleges will have 20,000, while teacher training colleges will have 35,000. The expanded market should attract local commercial publishers, particularly in view of the growing government monopoly of the primary and secondary school market.

Of the four public universities, Nairobi, Moi, Kenyatta, and Egerton, only Nairobi has a university press. It was set up seven years ago with a sizable grant from British American Tobacco. Up to now, it has only published one title, a sign that all is not well within its management.

Prospects for future publishing in this area appear bright. Apart from commercial publishers and a revitalized University of Nairobi Press, two new publishers, Academy Science Publishers and African Centre for Technology Studies Press have emerged and show every sign of being able to produce high-quality university textbooks. To facilitate the success of the university publishing program, it would be a good idea if the government and university authorities would ensure that student loans intended for the purchase of textbooks are indeed utilized for this purpose.

JOURNALS

Journals are extremely important as a forum for exchanging peer views on the latest developments in the world of knowledge. We shall now conclude this section by having a brief look at the current journal-publishing situation in Kenya, even if it is to draw attention to the nonexistence of journals.

Most of the country's journals were launched in the period between 1965 and 1975. The *East African Journal*, started by the East African Institute of Social and Cultural Affairs, was among the early ones and was a major forum for academic discussion of burning issues of the day. *East African Economic Review*, *Zuka*, and *Azania* were started by EALB and, in line with its policy, handed over to Oxford University Press for commercial exploitation, which eventually discontinued them on account of being nonviable.

By the mid-1970s, there were close to 30 academic journals published, mostly by the EALB and EAPH. Nearly all these journals stopped in 1977 when the bureau folded up and the local publishing industry started experiencing problems, as discussed earlier. The death of EAPH itself, in 1987, put the final nail in the coffin of journal publishing in Kenya. Now that the KLB is profitable, perhaps it should give some thought to reviving some of these journals to facilitate the much-needed academic exchange of ideas. Credit must be given to Gideon S. Were Press for initiating and continuing to publish two journals, the *Journal of Eastern African Research and Development* and the *Trans-African Journal of History*, even in these difficult times. The newly launched *Innovation and Discovery*, by the Academy Science Publishers, will fill a gap long felt by all scientists in Africa, who hitherto had no forum for exchanging their new ideas and discoveries.

PRESENT AND FUTURE CHALLENGES

Earlier, we traced the beginnings and development of the Kenyan publishing industry from independence to the present. In part two, we attempted to analyze the composition of this industry from a thematic point of view, highlighting output from each subject area. In this third and last section, we shall discuss the reasons for the strengths and weaknesses of each subject area and attempt to make proposals as to what action should be taken to streamline and strengthen the industry. As we have seen, the textbook market is overpublished, while the fiction, children's books, adult literacy, general books, academic, technical and reference books, and journal subject areas remain largely undeveloped.

Government Policies

There is no government policy today that controls, regulates, coordinates, and stabilizes the overall behavior of the industry. We have closely studied the various Education Commission reports since independence, from the Ominde Report of 1964 to the Kamunge Report of 1988, and can find no proposal for policy guidelines for the book industry. The reports tend to discuss the procurement and distribution of books and other educational materials as if they are already there. The Gachathi Report describes the book publishing process at length but makes no attempt to comment on the book industry itself.[6] Perhaps it is the Kamunge Report that comes closest when it says:

> To help schools obtain textbooks readily the Kenya Institute of Education, Jomo Kenyatta Foundation and the Kenya Literature Bureau have been given the responsibility to prepare and publish them. . . . The Working Party, however, notes the need for the production of supplementary reading materials. In this respect, Kenyan writers and publishers should be encouraged to produce such additional reading materials.[7]

Commenting on the failure of the adult literacy program, the commission acknowledges the "non-availability of appropriate reading materials in some ethnic languages," and emphasizes the need to "develop reading materials in various ethnic languages to enhance literacy among literate adults."[8] It is not clear who is being called upon to develop and publish these reading materials. The two state-supported publishers—EALB and EAPH—who previously published such materials, are no longer in business, and no attempt has been made to transfer these vital functions to some other government institution. The new KLB, which could have inherited this role from EALB, is now a mainstream commercial publisher with a monopoly to publish textbooks for schools. Only the mission presses are producing primers, which, though intended primarily for church purposes, are useful to adult literacy learners.

At the moment, the Kenyan publishing industry is lopsided and unbalanced. Instead of providing services, the government has, through its parastatals, gone full blast into trading in books, employing the public infrastructure to push out commercial publishers. The fortunes and misfortunes of the industry fluctuate with regular ministerial and civil service directives from the Ministry of Education, some of them ambiguous, even contradictory. If the industry is to settle down and develop, it should be guided like other industries in the country by an act of Parliament, with the roles and functions of the various types of publishers operating in the market clearly defined. In particular, it should highlight the relationship envisaged between commercial and state publishers and how these are to coexist. The hostility of some Ministry of Education officials toward commercial publishers makes it appear that the latter are not wanted. If commercial publishers are perceived as not playing a useful role, they should be told so, so that they can look for other forms of livelihood.

The Language Dilemma

Kenya has a complicated language situation. Every indigenous Kenyan is exposed to at least three languages: English, Kiswahili, and a mother tongue. The English language was brought by British colonialists at the turn of the last century. Kiswahili, a Bantu language of the Swahili people of Kenya's coastal area, has been used as the language of trade between the coastal and inland peoples of Kenya and beyond for many years. There are reported to be over 40 ethnic languages in Kenya. Before independence, English was the "national" language, but Kiswahili and the mother tongues were not suppressed. Many settlers learned to speak Kiswahili; missionaries learned the mother tongues of the areas in which they operated and managed to formulate orthographies and to publish materials in those languages. English was the language of education, and every African who went to school was able to speak it. This was the confused language situation in the country at independence; the new government had to do something about it.

In 1964, the Ominde Commission was appointed to undertake an exhaustive inquiry into all aspects of education in Kenya. On the matter of language policy, the commission, which had received views from a cross section of members of the public reported that "the great majority of witnesses wished to see the universal use of the English language as the medium of instruction from Primary 1" and proceeded to give their reasons as follows:

> First, the English medium makes possible a systematic development of language study and literacy which would be very difficult to achieve in the vernaculars. Secondly, as a result of the sys-

tematic development possible in the English medium, quicker progress is possible in all subjects. Thirdly, the foundation laid in the first three years is more scientifically conceived, and therefore provides a more solid basis for all subsequent studies, than was ever possible in the old vernacular teaching. Fourthly, the difficult transition from a vernacular to an English medium, which can take up much time in Primary V, is avoided. Fifthly, the resulting linguistic equipment is expected to be much more satisfactory, an advantage that cannot fail to expedite and improve the quality of post-primary education of all kinds. Lastly, advantage has been taken of the new medium to introduce modern infant techniques into the first three years, including activity and group work and a balanced development of muscular coordination. In short, we have no doubt about the advantages of the English medium to the whole educational process.[9]

About Kiswahili, the commission reported that

those giving evidence were virtually unanimous in recommending a general spread of this language, not only to provide an additional and specifically African vehicle for national coordination and unification, but also to encourage communication on an international basis, not only within East Africa, but also with the Eastern parts of the Congo and parts of Central Africa. Kiswahili is, therefore, recognized both as a unifying national influence and as a means of Pan-African communication over a considerable part of the continent. In view of these important findings, we believe that Kiswahili should be a compulsory subject in the primary school.[10]

As far as "vernacular" languages are concerned, the commission's views were mixed, although there was the general feeling that one or two periods per day should be devoted to "vernacular" languages in all primary schools. This was followed up by a circular from the chief inspector of schools in 1965 reminding all schools of the importance of teaching African languages as a subject.

The Ominde Report, in effect, tried to accommodate the three language categories at once, but with varying degrees of emphasis. English was to be the medium of instruction, while Kiswahili and mother tongues were to become compulsory teaching subjects in the Kenyan school system.

The adoption of the report led to the launching of the New Primary Approach (NPA) in 1965, whose hallmark was the introduction of English from the very first day a pupil entered school. However, by 1967, it was found that schools, especially those in the rural areas, were experiencing difficulty with NPA, and most of them had, in fact, resorted to teaching in mother tongues. The government was thus compelled to withdraw NPA and allow the use of mother tongue languages during the first two or three years of primary school, and this is what is still happening today.

There have been no other statements on language policy in Kenya, except the designation of English as the "official" language and of Kiswahili, since 1977, as the "national" language. Unhappy with the present state of affairs, observers have complained that Kenya does not have a clear-cut language policy. Yet it is difficult to see an acceptable alternative to the existing arrangement. But strictly from the publishing point of view, it is an expensive policy and has had adverse effects on the publishing of school textbooks for Standard One to Three, children's books, and adult literacy materials, as ideally these have to be done in all three language categories if all Kenyans are to have access to them. English enjoys a special advantage over the other two. Not only is it a compulsory teaching subject right from Standard One, but other subjects are taught in it from Standard Four onward. It is the language used in official government correspondence and records, and its use still carries a certain amount of prestige in public life. In short, it is still seen as the language of the "properly educated."

A summary of new publications in Kiswahili, mother tongues, and English over the five-year period between 1985 and 1989 is given in Table 5. This shows that out of the 1,045 new titles that have been published, 777 titles (74 percent) were in English, while 219 titles (21 percent) were in Kiswahili, leaving mother tongue with a dismal 44 titles (4 percent), and others (1 percent). However, the statistics are different when one looks at the extent of use of these languages in oral communication.

In a survey published in a local paper, it was reported that 10 million Kenyans (65 percent) use Kiswahili in their day-to-day activities, while only 2.7 million (18 percent), use English.[11] Mother tongues are, of course, exclusively used by those who speak them, but the users are unlikely to be more than 20 percent of the total population, since Kenya's largest ethnic group, the Gikuyu, are estimated to be about 20 percent of Kenya's population.

Table 5
Number of Titles According to Language of Publication

	1985	1986	1987	1988	1989	Totals
National Languages						
Swahili	28	38	30	54	69	219
Others	2	5	3	9	25	44
Foreign Languages						
English	82	110	161	161	263	777
Others	3	—	—	—	2	5
Totals	115	153	194	224	359	1,045

English and Kiswahili will continue to be used side by side for a long time to come. Kiswahili will increasingly enter into the education system—it is now a compulsory subject at primary, secondary, and teachers' colleges level—while English will widen its constituency in oral communication. In Nairobi and other urban centers, the two have already merged to produce a new "highbreed" language called "Sheng."

ILLITERACY

Illiteracy is, without doubt, the greatest challenge facing the book industry in Kenya today. It has exercised the minds of educational experts since independence, and recommendation after recommendation has been made for its eradication. But the government's achievement in this area has been nothing compared to the success in the formal-education sector. The 1969 census gave the rate of illiteracy as 73 percent. In the 1979 census, this figure had come down to 51 percent—it is claimed, largely as a result of efforts in the formal-education sector. Official reports say that the current rate is 53 percent. But it is difficult to determine the accuracy of these statements. As late as 1988, the Kamunge Commission, like all others before it, was recommending a survey to establish the extent of adult illiteracy in Kenya.

The Board of Adult Education is the organ charged with the responsibility of fighting illiteracy in Kenya. It employs 3,000 full-time adult education teachers, 5,000 paid part-time, and about 5,000 part-time volunteer teachers. The latter two categories consist of untrained teachers, many of whom are irregular in attending to their work, which is discouraging to their adult learners. But even if all were trained and took their jobs seriously, they would still be too few to deal with the mammoth task of rescuing several million people from illiteracy. Generally, the program suffers from half-hearted commitment from the government, coupled with lack of incentives to the adult learners, lack of funds to recruit adequate and qualified teachers, and nonavailability of appropriate reading materials, among other things.

An adult literacy campaign can only succeed if it is intensively done over a period of, say, two to three years. During this period, all available resources should be mobilized under the direction of a mass movement such as a political party. Regular teachers, retired teachers, and university students should be recruited to reinforce existing manpower and the support of the administration and public media enlisted to popularize the program. Books and other reading materials should be an essential part of this exercise, and in the follow-up exercise of reading for continuing and lifelong education to prevent the new literates from lapsing back into illiteracy.

In the absence of the services previously provided in this area by the former EALB and, to lesser extent, EAPH, a new institution should be created or an existing one redesignated to publish in this area. Alternatively, the board should be given adequate funds and enabled to publish these materials with the assistance of a willing publisher—of which there are many. If this is not done, universal adult literacy by the year 2000 must be accepted as a chimera. It is a pity that more than 25 years after independence, a very large number of Kenyans are still locked out of the secrets contained in a book and are thus unable to participate fully in the development of their nation. If Tanzania can achieve a literacy rate of 85 percent, as has been reported, then Kenya, which has more resources, can manage the same, if not more!

READING

Kenyans have been known not to read beyond completion of their formal education. This is largely true of the older generation, which was brought up under the British colonial education system. That system emphasized education for achievement rather than education for life. These people were made to read irrelevant books (mostly of a religious nature) in which they had little or no interest. They were induced and motivated with promises of material and spiritual rewards—a good job, prestige, financial gain, and a comfortable life at the end of their "reading." In the end, those who attained these rewards stopped reading because there was nothing more to read for, and those who did not attain them stopped reading out of frustration. This attitude was carried on through generations and still lingers in the minds of some Kenyans today.

Cultural factors also have a negative effect on reading. African people, in general, derive more pleasure and communicate more easily through the oral and performing arts—talking, singing, dancing, music, and drama. Communication through the book is a private undertaking, the pursuit of which alienates the reader from his or her own community, whose best form of entertainment comes through participation in communal activities. Communication through a book is a one-way process that many Kenyans find useless and boring. This attitude may be due, in part, to the kind of books that Kenyans have been exposed to so far. Many of them do not appeal to the particular and daily concerns of Kenyans and are mostly written in English, a foreign language accessible to less than 20 percent of the country's population. Furthermore, most of the mother tongue languages do not have developed orthographies, so that even when books are written in them, the characters on the page do not always conform to the sounds intended, making the reading difficult and helping further to alienate readers from a language they know so well.

We have already discussed illiteracy as a major handicap to reading and have touched briefly on reasons why Kenyans do not read. We must now turn our attention to those Kenyans who want to read but cannot get access to books. As pointed out elsewhere, school libraries are few and poorly stocked. Home libraries are almost nonexistent. Bookshops are located only in the main urban centers, so that it is difficult to find books in the rural areas. There are other Kenyans who do want to read but cannot afford to do so. In a survey conducted by local newspapers and magazine firms, it was found that sales represented only 10 percent of the total readership.[12] This pattern is also true of books. In a survey conducted by this writer on the reading habits of Nairobi schoolchildren, and compiled at the National Academy for the Advancement of Arts and Sciences, nearly 36 percent of the children interviewed reported that they had borrowed the book they were reading from a friend, while 34 percent had borrowed from a library. Only 20 percent had bought the book they were reading, so it is as much a book-buying as a book-reading problem.[13]

Thus one cannot rule out economic considerations as contributing to the low reading levels. Kenya's average per capita income in 1988 was U.S.$300. Many people, both in rural and urban areas, are struggling to earn enough to meet the bare necessities of life—food, shelter, clothing. It would be unrealistic to expect such people to consider book buying or book reading a worthwhile undertaking. A general rise in the people's living standards would bring with it spare cash and more leisure time—some of which might be expended on books.

The challenge to get many more Kenyans to read must be accepted by all. Publishers complain that they are only able to sell an average of 1,000 copies of a successful local book of fiction. They must be encouraged to continue publishing in this area and assisted to carry out research to ascertain the real reading interests of their audiences. It is clear that Kenyans would buy books in much larger quantities than the figure mentioned above if the books appealed to them in some special way. Books such as Charles Mangua's *Son of Woman*, David Maillu's *After 4:30*, Ngugi wa Thiong'o's *Caitani Mutharaba-ini*, John Kariamiti's *My Life in Crime*, Ochieng' and Karimi's *The Kenyatta Succession*, and Pat Ngurukie's *Soldier's Wife* have sold in large numbers, with additional printings within the first few months of publication. In the survey referred to earlier, agreeing that the reading materials available were generally unsuitable, the children expressed the wish to see more comics, fiction, biographies, and sport books made available for their reading. They reported that they came from crowded homes or lived with relatives in conditions not conducive to reading. Some of them lived in houses without electricity, and others were made to do housework after school and could not find time to read. The sentiments voiced by Nairobi school children are even more acutely felt by children in rural areas. A reading environment must be created and sustained. More school and public libraries should be set up. We believe simple reading rooms scattered in rural areas would be more effective than the imposing public libraries presently being built on a per district basis. Reading education should be introduced in schools and reading competitions held regularly in order to sustain interest in the subject. At home, those parents who are able to read should make it their responsibility to read to their children every night. Children who have grown up with reading will develop into habitual adult readers.

Writing

As late as the early 1970s, all textbooks used in the Kenyan school system were written by foreigners. With the advent of the 8-4-4 education system launched five years ago, a dramatic change has taken place. New textbooks developed at KIE using local personnel now dominate the market. These textbooks were written in record time by panels consisting of subject experts drawn from all over the country. Most of the alternative textbooks from commercial publishers have invariably been written by locals. It would appear, therefore, that for the time being, Kenya is self-sufficient in the areas of primary and secondary school textbook writers.

But the same cannot be said of other areas such as fiction, academic, reference and technical books, adult-literacy, general, and children's books. Auxiliary cadres such as illustrators, designers, and paste-up artists are hard to come by. Translators, critical in a multilingual situation such as Kenya, are rare. Those people are there, but they need to be properly educated about publishing and given training and encouragement if they are to succeed. A lot of them are not familiar with publishing practices. They prepare their manuscripts in isolation and only bring them to the publisher when they are complete. Such authors should be advised to visit publishers, discuss their plans, obtain the publishers' approval and guidelines in the preparation of their manuscripts to ensure that the end product is publishable.

It is true to say that Kenyan writers do not enjoy public esteem and are not given incentives that would encourage them to make writing a career. Until recently, the KIE panel writers were given neither a royalty nor honorarium. Once committed to KIE, they are still not allowed to write for commercial publishers and therefore have few chances of developing into full-blown self-motivated textbook writers. Our view is that once freed from their KIE obligations, these teachers should be allowed to enhance their newly acquired skills in writing as widely as possible and for a publisher of their choice. Their teaching load should be reduced, instead of the current practice where they are promoted to administrative positions such as headmaster, inspector, or education officer. They should be allowed to continue to maintain contact with the classroom so as to remain in touch with the students for whom they are writing the books. But their terms of service should be considered for additional incentives such as fully paid-up lecture tours, fellowships, longer leave, research funds, income-tax relief on royalty earnings, and so on. They might also be considered for Presidential Awards in recognition of their service to the country.

A national award scheme should be set up so that writers whose books excel in any one year can win prizes, especially in the areas of fiction, children's, and academic books. The Jomo Kenyatta Prize of Literature, inaugurated in 1972 by the Kenya Publishers Association, may have contributed toward the burst of creativity in Kenya in the period that immediately followed it. Sadly, this prize died away after only six years because the association was without funds and lacked the unity, strength, or will to find a new sponsor. So, for the last 12 years there has been no literary prize on the local scene to stimulate the minds of local fiction writers. The Noma Award for Publishing in Africa has been widely publicized in the country and has given hopes of international recognition to many Kenyan writers. In 1981, Kenya's longest-serving author and publisher, Gakaara wa Wanjua, won the prize with his prison diary *Mwandiki Wa Mau Mau Ithamirio-ini*, written in the Gikuyu language and published by Heinemann Kenya. Such incentives can stimulate and encourage existing and new writers to rise to the challenge of writing more books for both educational and leisure reading.

PUBLISHING

Previously, the real problem with the Kenyan publishing industry was that it was dominated by multinationals. But over the last five years, things have changed somewhat. Two of the largest commercial publishers, Longman Kenya and Heinemann Kenya, have come under the control of locals. Their next challenge is to fully "Kenyanize" their lists, a portion of which are now still written, developed, and printed out of the country. The next goal will be to get the public and government to "accept" them as national publishing institutions. They currently suffer from an identity crisis that in the current uncertain market conditions is likely to persist for some time yet.

We have already said elsewhere that the industry lacks government guidelines to regulate its behavior. In such an unsteady environment it is unlikely that publishers can indulge in expensive and long-term projects. They prefer to operate in the safe textbook market, where immediate returns are assured. Unless they make sacrifices and agree to stretch their investment over longer periods, key publishing areas are likely to remain neglected for a long time. Already Phoenix and Heinemann Kenya are showing that it is possible to publish children's books profitably. With the support of the recently established African Books Collection, Kenyan books will find new markets in Europe and North America and these difficult publishing subject areas will become a little less risky.

The industry currently suffers from lack of trained personnel in vital areas such as editing, designing, proofreading, and marking-up a book. Awareness of the lack of personnel in the information industry led to the creation of a Faculty of Information Sciences at Moi University. Since 1991, the flow of journalists, librarians, archivists, editors, and others from this institution is helping to ensure that the needs of the industry will be more adequately served. Even then, it will be necessary to have regular seminars and on-the-job training for these people and others entering the industry at some other level.

But the greatest problem facing Kenyan publishers is the lack of capital. This problem is felt more acutely by the small indigenous publishers. A book can take up to two years from the time of commissioning an author to write it to the time of finished copies, and might take longer to sell. The publisher's money would normally be locked up in new projects (for which he has nothing to show) and stock that may or may not be selling. The risk factor is great, since no publisher, however good, can predict with any degree of certainty how many copies of a new book will sell. Banks in Kenya are reluctant to lend to publishers and will not accept stock as security. The track record of the industry, with a trail of bankruptcies behind it, it checkered, to say the least.

Against this background, the new loan-guarantee scheme for local publishers, initiated by the Dag Hammarskjold Foundation has been greeted with relief. Already a number of publishers have benefited from it. Already, hitherto dormant ones are showing signs of awakening, and new ones are emerging. Among those who have benefited from the scheme is Gakaara wa Wanjau, the veteran freedom fighter, who, since the early 1950s, has been publishing readers and primers in the Gikuyu language. Another is David Maillu, formerly of Comb Books, but who has reemerged with a new company, Maillu Publishing House, in which he is publishing some of his own fiction and other educational materials. Other beneficiaries have been Waruingi Gacheche of Phoenix Publishers and Asenath Odaga, who operates out of Nairobi and publishes children's books and fiction in both English and Dholuo. These are difficult publishing areas indeed and the loan-guarantee scheme will help such publishers cope with the expected cash-flow problems. Another publisher in this group is Sylvester Ouma, whose company, Shirikon, publishes mainly in the area of cooperatives. And lastly are Pete Ondeng of Enterprises Publications, who has broken into the market with the successful title *How to Start Your Own Small Business* and Stanley Irura of Bookman Consultants, publisher of the *Kenyan Bookseller* and organizers of the last two Nairobi Book Fairs. If sympathetically administered and responsibly utilized, the scheme represents a major breakthrough that in time could change the face of the publishing industry in Kenya.

Finally, the large Kenyan publishers are not enterprising enough; they do not want to stray from the beaten track. They would be well advised to look out for new opportunities in mother tongue publishing and in other areas such as coeditions with foreign publishers—from whom they might secure local reprint rights, adaptations rights, translation rights, and so on. Heinemann Kenya appears to be the only one doing this; the rest should take up the challenge.

PRICING

Over the last few years, there has been a hue and cry, especially from government officials and parents, over the pricing of books in Kenya. Firstly, at an average price of U.S.$2.00 for a primary school textbook and U.S.$3.50 for a secondary school book, it can be argued that these prices are most reasonable. However, this is not so in Kenyan shilling terms. Over the last two years, the shilling has lost 50 percent of its value against international currencies. In the same period, the Panafrican Paper Mill, at Webuye, has increased the price of its paper by 40 percent, citing the cost of debt servicing and the increasing price of oil as the main reasons. Consequently, publishers have had to increase their prices by between 30 and 40 percent over the same period, since paper contributes nearly 65 percent of the cost of producing a book.

Textbooks published by state parastatals are, on the whole, 20 to 30 percent cheaper. This is because they do not pay royalties, and some of their costs are borne by government. As monopolies, their advertising, promotional, marketing, and distribution costs are minimal. In sum, state-published books are cheaper because they are subsidized by the taxpayer. Commercial publishers have had to adjust to the reality of printing fewer and fewer of their textbooks, which have to compete with state publications. And, as economies of scale would have it, commercial publishers have had to pay higher unit costs, and adjust their prices accordingly.

It is not possible to publish cheap books in Kenya without government subsidies. One cannot print on cheaper paper because it does not exist. Of the local paper mill's yearly capacity of 100,000 tons, less than 5,000 tons is book paper. The government could arrange with the paper mill to sell subsidized book paper or grant certain rebates on paper sold to the local book industry, as has indeed happened before. Further, government could lower the corporation tax and introduce special tax benefits for publishers. All these measures could bring down the prices of books by as much as 40 percent in the same year they were introduced.

DISTRIBUTION

Before we can deal with distribution per se, let us look briefly at the means employed in creating book awareness in Kenya. Publishers prepare catalogs and stocklists and mail these out to schools and other catchment points. They also send their salesmen to these places to exhibit new and backlist titles for possible adoption. On special occasions, such as the opening of a new school term, publishers may advertise their books in local newspapers and magazines. The *Voice of Kenya* has a weekly radio program entitled "Books and Bookmen," during which new books (mostly fiction) are discussed by individual critics or panels. Sometimes, authors are invited to read their own works and share their experiences with the listening public. Occasionally, outstanding local authors are invited to special programs or even press conferences on radio or television. Book reviews in the press and radio are not uncommon. On the whole, it is our view that books are accorded sufficient publicity and promotion in Kenya.

But the methods of getting books to the consumer could be improved. The postal system is slow and still expensive in spite of the special book tariffs in operation. Bookshops are still very few and concentrated in the urban centers. We must reemphasize, though, that since the KSES was discontinued six years ago, the number of bookshops in the country has increased twofold from 200 to 400. And, with more surveillance from the Kenya Booksellers and Stationers Association, augmented by the current practice of publishers' printing book prices on covers, the big markups that used to give bookselling a bad name are gradually disappearing. Now it is possible to buy books at the recommended prices in bookshops far away from Nairobi. Bookshops are certainly becoming a key link in the book distribution chain, and more incentives should be given to entrepreneurs wishing to set up bookshops, particularly in the rural areas.

Part of the function of the now-defunct EALB was "to establish and administer a lending library service for African readers." To achieve this aim, EALB launched a library system in the 1950s that provided the people of East Africa with access to books through postal borrowing and mobile book vans, while plans for the building of libraries in selected centers were being worked out. At the attainment of independence in 1963, the library division of EALB became the Kenya National Library Services (KNLS).

Today, KNLS, with a chain of branch libraries in Eldoret, Embu, Garissa, Kakamega, Kisumu, Mombasa, Nakuru, Meru, Kabarnet, Nyeri, Thika, Kericho, and Kisii, is the largest and most extensive library network in the country. It also operates seven mobile libraries, which ply the remote areas of the country, visiting rural centers, lending out books and advising on their use. KNLS plans to have a library in each of Kenya's 40 districts by the year 2000. Other public libraries are to be found in Nairobi and half a dozen municipal towns. We have already observed that the libraries currently being built are far too expensive and tend to overwhelm the rural folk into thinking that they were not meant for them. They have so far failed to attract the general or for-pleasure reader. Instead, they appear to serve as extension libraries to surrounding schools or as substitutes for those schools that have none. Most people would be content with a simple reading room where they could stop to read daily newspapers, magazines, and to borrow the odd book. It would be possible to reach more people and in more places if our concept of a library were to be adapted to our particular circumstances. The overriding principle should be to spend more money buying books rather than putting up elaborate structures.

On the whole, Kenyan books are reasonably well distributed internally, although they could benefit from the existence of more bookshops and libraries. But when it comes to regional and overseas markets, the situation is completely different. There is a lot of demand for Kenyan books in neighboring markets such as Uganda, Tanzania, and Southern Sudan, but this cannot be met because of a shortage of foreign exchange in those countries. The World Bank would be well advised to look at what is available in Kenya first before turning to the United Kingdom for fulfillment of their IDA projects in Uganda and Tanzania. The launching of the Preferred Trade Agreement (PTA) was received with considerable relief by member countries in the region. Its effects have been felt in sections of the Kenyan manufacturing sector. Trade in books has yet to be included, but we are hoping that this will come sooner or later so that Kenyan books can be exported to Zimbabwe, Zambia, Malawi, and the rest of Southern Africa, where they are also reported to be in demand. Distributing Kenyan books to the rest of Africa still remains a major challenge.

There has been a major breakthrough in the distribution of African-published books to Western Europe and America. A group of African publishers has launched African Books Collective (ABC), a new company that is to promote and distribute their books in Europe, North America, and in Commonwealth countries. The company, which is based in Oxford, U.K., started operations in 1990. ABC will not only ease the burden of African publishers wishing to sell abroad, but also that of European and American libraries, which have been facing chronic problems in the acquisition of African publications. Unfortunately, only one Kenyan publisher is a member of the collective. Other publishers would be well advised to become part of this self-help initiative as it is likely to have a major impact on their sales, particularly of their children's, fiction, general, and academic lists.

CONCLUSION

In this study, we have attempted to analyze the Kenyan publishing industry as it is, highlighting its strengths and weaknesses and suggesting how best to solve its problems. The industry can only be independent if it is fully owned and controlled by Kenyans and if it projects and is seen to project a truly Kenyan image locally and abroad. As we have seen, there are certain aspects in which it is independent and others in which it still depends on foreign products and inputs. The localization of Longman and Heinemann is a move that other foreign-controlled publishers should emulate.

The fact that the country still imports 40 percent of its book needs is a matter of concern. Academic, technical, and reference books should and will continue to be imported for as long as local publishers do not have the capability to publish them or as long as the numbers do not make it viable to develop them locally. But every attempt should be made to ensure that local reprint licenses are obtained on all foreign textbooks used in primary and secondary schools so that these are published locally. An export drive should be launched with a view to selling Kenyan books in the neighboring markets and the PTA region as a whole, with the aim of raising the value of exports to that of imports, as was the case in 1976 just before the collapse of the East African Community. Only then can the Kenyan publishing industry claim to be independent.

This target can be achieved if certain assumptions are met. The first concerns a continuation of the same conditions that exist today— a vibrant printing industry and continuous availability of book paper from the local paper mill. The second requires that government is willing to cooperate on the various issues raised in this study and acts to provide an enabling environment on the local market, particularly by discontinuing the present monopoly enjoyed by the state parastatals and reducing the price of book paper. The third assumption is that professional associations within the book industry will be strengthened and work closely with each other so that matters affecting their welfare can be brought to the attention of government and the public at large in a forceful and united manner. Indeed, the Book Development Council proposed earlier would provide an ideal communication forum between the government and the book industry, the latter represented by the professional associations. The fourth assumption is that the industry, already fully Kenyanized, will be manned by trained book professionals who are able to provide the management skills that are crucial to the success of any enterprise. If these things are attended to, the Kenyan publishing industry, already one of the most active in sub-Saharan Africa, will grow stronger and more independent than it is today.

2

Private Enterprise Publishing in Kenya: A Long Struggle for Emancipation

The market for books in Kenya today is about 800 million Kenyan shillings (about U.S.$10 million). Kiswahili is the national language, although most of the publishing is in English, the official language and medium of instruction in schools. The country has more than 600 bookshops, ten good-quality printers, and a paper mill that supplies the nation's basic needs. The transport system by road, rail, air, and sea is adequate. The postal system is reasonably reliable and fast and is supplemented by private carriers. The telephone system works most of the time and is one of the best in Africa. There are seven million school-going children out of the national population of twenty-four million. Kiswahili is spoken in neighboring countries (Uganda and Tanzania), so there is scope for exports.

Kenyan book publishers thus enjoy an exceptionally conducive environment by African standards. Yet, local private enterprise publishing has not flourished. About 40 percent of all publishing is done by the state. Imports from 20 percent and religious presses supply 10 percent. Most of the remaining 30 percent is in the hands of foreign-owned publishers. Since Kenya became independent in 1963, the indigenous publisher has been squeezed uneasily between his own government and the Kenyan branches of mulitnational companies. Emancipation is now in sight. It has been a long struggle. Why and how that struggle took place, and my own experience of it, illustrate the uncertain path of book development in the postcolonial world. Paved with good intentions, it is a path, in Kenya as in many other countries, subject to twists, turns, rocks, hard places, and pitfalls.

From *Logos* (1993).

Historical Background

Local book publishing in Kenya can be traced as far back as 1894 when the Christian Missionary Society issued its first book. It remained in the hands of missions for most of the first half of the twentieth century and was mainly concerned with schoolbooks. In the 1940s, the mission presses came together and formed Ndia Kuu Press, a commercial venture to publish not only schoolbooks, but adult literacy materials and fiction, especially in African languages. This venture fizzled out in 1947 when its manager was appointed to an organization set up by the East African governments (Kenya, Tanzania, and Uganda). Called the East Africa Literature Bureau (EALB), this body had a similar mission to that of Ndia Kuu. It is not known how many books Ndia Kuu published, as some of them were taken over by other publishers. *Highway Arithmetic*, published today by Longman, appears to have been originated by Ndia Kuu.

The large British educational publishing houses began to take an interest in Kenya in the early 1950s. Longman and Oxford University Press (OUP) were the first to appoint local representatives, whose jobs were both to sell their principals' lists and to scout for manuscripts, which they forwarded to their head offices for possible publication. The government's EALB itself was a major source of such manuscripts, as it was official policy to seek commercial exploitation of successful books and journals. Soon after Kenya became independent in 1963, the Longman and OUP agencies were upgraded to full branches and locally incorporated. Other British companies, including Heinemann, Macmillan, Evans, Nelson, Pitman, and Cambridge University Press, followed suit. Other companies that where not basically schoolbook publishers, such as Collins, McGraw-Hill, or Edward Arnold, set up agencies. Each branch or agency represented other publishers so that by the mid 1970s, approximately ninety publishers, mainly British, had a presence in the country.

Between 1963 and 1977, about ten local publishers attempted to establish themselves. They were up against not only the multinationals, but also the Kenyan government. It was fashionable after independence for African governments to nationalize important sectors of the economy and create state institutions to take charge on a monopoly or near monopoly basis. This happened, for example, in Ghana, Uganda, Tanzania, and Zambia, where it became virtually impossible for commercial publishing to develop after independence. Kenya was an exception. Instead of nationalization, a curriculum development center, the Kenya Institute of Education (KIE), was created in 1964. Its duty was to develop suitable syllabuses for the new Kenya and to develop course materials for the new curricula. The following year, the Jomo Kenyatta Foundation was established, more as a charity than a commercial organization, to publish primary school materials developed by KIE. At this stage, it was possible for commercial publishers to reach agreements to publish materials for and on behalf of these two institutions. Houses such as Longman or OUP took advantage of this facility.

Also in 1965, a new publishing house was formed by the East African Cultural Trust, a group of East and Central African intellectuals, supported by their mother countries and donor funds. Called the East African Publishing House (EAPH), its ambition was to establish an outlet for the academic and creative output of the members of the Trust, which they claimed was being ignored by foreign publishers.

Although some publishing institutions were thus formed with government help, mainstream publishing was left largely in the hands of commercial publishers, most of which were local branches of multinationals. The fact that the Kenyan government did not nationalize the publishing industry at the time of independence enabled commercial publishing to develop.

By 1977, Nairobi had become the enviable educational, cultural, and publishing center of East Africa. The University of Nairobi was bustling with such luminaries as Ngugi Wa Thiong'o, Okot p' Bitek, Taban lo Liyong, Owuor Anyumba, Micere Mugo, Joe de Graft, Jared Angira, and Francis Imbuga, to name only a few. Elsewhere, new writers such as Charles Mangua, David Maillu, Meja Mwangi, Mwangi Ruheni, Sam Kahiga, and John Ruganda were coming up, each with his own brand of fiction. A few local publishers who had established themselves on the scene, such as Comb Books and Foundation Books, were thriving on their own brand of literature and had started exporting some of their Kiswahili publications to Tanzania. British publishers were humming in and out by the dozen.

In 1977, the East African Community consisting of Kenya, Uganda, and Tanzania, collapsed. The prosperity of Kenyan publishing had depended to some extent on a common curriculum set by the East African Examination Council. The loss of the Ugandan and Tanzanian markets and the need to develop new textbooks for Kenya's amended syllabi sent small publishers such as Comb and Foundation into bankruptcy. The stream of British visitors dried up. The branches of Longman and OUP retrenched. It took several years for the industry to adjust to the new scenario and it has not fully recovered to this date. Recent moves to restore trade among the former community members could boost commercial publishing in all three territories.

Also in 1977, there was a dangerous development, not publicized, which, had it succeeded, would have changed the face of commercial publishing in Kenya. The government, through the Kenya Schools Equipment Scheme (KSES), had, as usual, advertised its annual tender for books. Also as usual, all commercial publishers whose books were on the tender had sent in their bids. Later, we came to learn that the whole tender had been awarded to one local publisher and that it was the government's wish that all orders be supplied through this publisher, who was very well connected in government at that time. Through the KPA, a delegation of publishers sought an urgent meeting with the minister for education and after much pestering, got an appointment one late afternoon. Much to our disappointment, we found the minister seated with his permanent secretary, whom we suspected of complicity. After a tedious argument with the permanent secretary, touching on such issues as irregular procedures, copyright infringements, delays, and all sorts of logistical complications, the diminutive minister, who had said nothing up to this point, pushed his glasses up his forehead and said philosophically: "As I understand it, you gentlemen have been on a hunt, in the forest, and you have returned home with a fat antelope. You have skinned it and are just about to roast it when another gentleman comes along with a knife. . . ."

"Mr. Minister," exclaimed one of the expatriates on our delegation, "this is a serious matter and should be treated with the seriousness it deserves. Hunting may be risky, but is nowhere as complicated as publishing. We want an answer from you." But the minister, perhaps upset at not being allowed to finish his analogy, went no further.

We met afterwards and agreed not to supply our books through the favored publisher and wrote a long letter to the minister stating our position. That year, the schools went without our books, but we were delighted to see the following words on the tender documents for the next year: "Only publishers or their authorized representatives may quote for their books." Once more an attempt to derail the progress of commercial publishing had been thwarted.

The Textbook War

A more serious setback occurred in 1985, when the country changed its educational system once more. The announcement that the new system was to be implemented without delay caught everyone, including publishers, by surprise. As the incumbent chairman of the Kenya Publishers Association, I wrote to the Ministry of Education seeking details of the new system and asking the ministry to publish the new syllabuses so that we could revise our textbooks or commission new ones. I received no reply, but at an official function around that time the minister announced that the writing of new textbooks was nearing completion at the KIE and that two state publishing houses, one formed after the collapse of the EALB, would be revitalized and awarded the publishing contract. The minister added further that, when published, these books would be the only materials recommended. The explanation of this volte-face was that Kenya had obtained a loan from the World Bank and the government had decided to use some of these funds to revive the two state publishing firms and operate them commercially, although neither had been set up for this purpose.

What followed, dubbed the "textbook war," was fought not only in publishers' boardrooms and government offices, but on the pages of the daily press. So intense was the debate that on occasions it commanded the front pages of our major daily newspapers and was the subject of their editorials. I argued that monopolies and state participation were against the spirit of the government's and the World Bank's stated policies of liberalization, free trade, and support for the private sector; that monopolies are inefficient and undermine the freedom of choice without which standards are bound to fall; that the chosen approach was not likely to be self-sustaining and that the government would find itself worse off at the end of the World Bank money; and that the state enterprise did not posses the expertise to enable it to produce the books to the required standard. When the first batch of publications came out, I condemned some of them as "sketchy, substandard and hurriedly put together." This last remark earned me a rebuke from the minister of education, who described me as "a multinational lackey, out for quick profits."

The "war" produced no winners and no losers. The debate had attracted participation from parents, teachers, pupils, and educational administrators, most of whom had insisted on being allowed to use books of their own choice. The press was sympathetic and regularly reported cases of teachers who had been harassed and threatened with punishment for using books that were not on the ministry's recommended list.

Finally, in the third year of the new system, the ministry started recommending books by commercial publishers, but only as "supplementary texts," "reference books," or "library books." This was because their own publishing program had left major gaps. Some of their books were weak. Others had suffered delays in production. Once again, commercial publishing had survived the onslaught, although the two state publishers had experienced tremendous growth in a very short time. Today, these two parastatals are publishing less and less as the effect of the World Bank money wears off and commercial publishers, who in the meantime have been publishing cautiously for the new curriculum, are poised to take the lead once more.

Through all these events, the indigenous local publishers were the losers. By 1987, most of them, including the EAPH, were bankrupt. There are many reasons why indigenous publishing has not taken off during the thirty years of Kenya's independence. In my view, the principal reason is that the government has never had a publishing policy or a book policy or even a broad information policy. Although it has adhered to the international conventions providing for copyright and the free flow of books, it has allowed multinationals to operate in the market freely and without any conditions or restrictions for far too long. On the other hand, it has itself attempted to dabble in commercial publishing at the expense of the local publishers. Sandwiched between the state and the multinationals, the local publisher, too weak to have a voice, has been squeezed into oblivion.

Personal Experiences

My own experience since August 1972, when I left my job as a tutor and postgraduate student in the Department of Philosophy and Religious Studies at the University of Nairobi to enter publishing, made me both a witness of and a participant in the frustrations of Kenya's short publishing history and points the way to a possible solution for private enterprise publishing.

The firm I joined was Heinemann, a venerable British imprint, which was already part of a multinational. Heinemann had established a company in Kenya in 1965 and by 1972 was ready to go into local publishing. Upon joining, my first reaction was disappointment. There were only five staff. Could this be "Heinemann East Africa"? I settled down uneasily, submitting to intensive formal and on-the-job training in Nairobi and London. By the beginning of 1974, I was put in charge of the publishing department and asked to develop a Kenyan publishing program. Hopes that I could nurture my writing skills and develop into an in-house author were soon dispelled, as I found myself endlessly writing other people's books for them. I had seen myself mingling with famous African writers, and in this respect I was not disappointed. I soon found myself rubbing shoulders with writers I had always wanted to meet, such as Achebe, Soyinka, Sembene Ousmane and Elechi Amadi, and at the same time recommending the work of many new ones for publication in the African Writers Series (AWS), which Heinemann had started in 1958.

In addition to reading and reporting for the AWS, I was able to launch two new imprints of a literary nature. The first was the Heinemann Students' Guides, which were intended to serve as an examination aid to literature students in their final year of secondary school. This series was suspiciously regarded, especially by my literary friends at the university, but when they saw the first few published titles, they realized that these were guides with a difference. The series, emulated by other local publishers, is still growing today, with more than fifty titles in print in both English and Kiswahili.

My other innovation was the Spear Books Series. When I realized that most of the AWS titles were fashioned for the classroom, I recommended to London, in 1973, that they should start a new series for leisure reading—romance, adventure, crime, etc.—as we were constantly receiving manuscripts of this kind. The idea was debated at length and turned down in 1974, but I was allowed to start such a series locally if I wished. The first four titles were launched in 1975 to much critical acclaim. Saleswise, they were modestly successful, but I continued with the series, which now has more than thirty titles in print and contains some of our bestselling fiction. Macmillan picked up this idea and launched their Pacesetters, gave them their full technical and marketing backup, and achieved instant success. By launching their African Heartbeat Series twenty years later, Heinemann has finally come round to accepting my advice, which, had it been implemented then, would have made them the single source of African creative writing in all its diversity. I also inherited a vigorous program of successful translations of AWS titles into Kiswahili. I continued with it for some time, but gradually slowed it down and eventually stopped it at the end of the 1970s, due to low sales, continuing to publish only the odd original work. The series has nearly forty titles in print.

There was greater success in the textbook market. I had much difficulty breaking into a market in which Longman and OUP had been active for a long time. My predecessor had acquired publishing rights to three geography textbooks developed by the Ministry of Education, Uganda. These kept us going for some time and I was able to add what turned out to be successful textbooks in English and Kiswahili. The breakthrough came with my adventure into primary school publishing. I decided to start with Kiswahili, a language to which the government was giving a lot of lip service, but which did not even have a detailed syllabus, let alone textbooks, especially at the primary level. Using the author of my successful secondary Kiswahili textbook (and against the advice of London, who insisted that Heinemann was and should remain a secondary school publisher), I embarked on this ambitious project in 1977. I had been appointed managing director of the company the previous year and was in a strong position to take some liberties. The first three textbooks came out in 1980 and were an instant success. The Ministry of Education's first order was for more than 100,000 copies of each and even included Books 4 and 5, which were not yet published! The series was completed the following year. Government orders continued pouring in. It is said that the textbook was used to draw up the current syllabus and this is why it is still having such a good run. We have followed up with textbooks in all the other primary school subjects, but none of them has been as successful. The ministry's change of policy in 1985 prevented these books from being recommended as mainline textbooks.

When I joined Heinemann East Africa in 1972, the entire revenue consisted of books published in the United Kingdom. By 1983, the local company was generating 80 percent of the turnover. There was a strong case for local equity. Agreement was reached to sell 60 pecent of the company to me and other Kenyan nationals. By the time this happened in 1985, imports were down to 15 percent and by 1992 to 8 percent. The company has returned profits every year since indigenization. The original investors have already recovered their initial investment almost twice over.

I was fortunate in being able to work under enlightened leadership. Without the help of Alan Hill, I doubt if indigenization could have been accomplished. The Heinemann management, I believe, genuinely wanted to turn their Kenyan company into a successful and independent African-owned publisher. They had allowed me to start publishing locally as soon as I joined and the freedom to choose what I wanted to publish, although this freedom was not absolute. They had helped finance my local publishing, through the current account, and had provided me with the production or marketing support whenever I needed it. Later, they had granted me sublicenses to reissue those titles whose principal market was East Africa and that could be reprinted locally in viable quantities. On the whole, my relationship with them has been entirely satisfactory and mutually symbiotic.

East African Educational Publishers (as the Heinemann company is now called) is not a typical case. Commercial publishing is, in the eyes of many Kenyans, still synonymous with foreign multinational publishing. Longman is planning to indigenize its company, but progress is held up by a dispute between its board and shareholders. The other major multinational players—OUP, Macmillan, and Evans—are still 100 percent foreign owned. I believe that my experience offers a possible model, not only for Kenya, but other countries, provided foreign publishers are willing, albeit under pressure, to indigenize their operations. Local publishing is the critical component. The emphasis within each house must be shifted from working through strong sales departments to building and developing publishing departments staffed with competent and well-trained editors. The long-term aim should be to encourage a strong local partner with whom, after indigenization, trade should continue. If the Longman deal goes through, pressure on the remaining foreign-owned houses is likely to mount and lead to some form of local participation, sooner or later. My only regret is that Heinemann, now part of Reed Elsevier, has not taken full advantage of our increased strength in the African marketplace to improve their promotion and distribution on the continent.

Conclusion

What is the future of private enterprise publishing in Kenya now? The intervention of the state in 1985 has proved to be temporary. With the reduction in World Bank funding, the state's role is likely to diminish gradually in the years ahead. It is unlikely that further World Bank loans, should they be forthcoming, will be used to prop up inefficient monopolies. This is now accepted as contrary to the spirit of free enterprise and privatization.

The multinationals, for their part, have passed their peak. Eventually, their local branches will either close down or be sold to local people. Book imports have suffered from adverse exchange rates and scarcity of foreign exchange. More British publishers are now trading directly with local book distributors, thus eliminating the overheads and inevitable markups of maintaining local branches.

The outlook for locally owned private enterprise publishing in Kenya is therefore brighter than in the past. Commercial publishing, in general, whether locally or foreign owned, could increase its share of the market to 50 percent in the next ten years, at the expense of the state, whose share would drop to 20 percent, while that of imports and mission presses would remain unchanged. This growth of commercial publishing will in due course include significant exports, which are now being developed for many African countries through the African Books Collective in Oxford.

Looking back twenty years and forward ten years, I see that the indispensable element for developing a publishing industry is a sound national book policy. Future policy is both to restrict and control the activities of foreign publishers when these do not contribute to local growth and also to create incentives for an indigenous publishing industry. Such a policy should also avoid creating and propping up parastatals in areas such as publishing. Ending multinational domination may require legislation, as has happened in Zimbabwe and Nigeria. My optimism about the future is based on the expectation that such a policy will come about and on my confidence that Kenya now has the financial and management expertise to develop on its own. There is, of course, one underlying assumption—that the country will continue to enjoy political stability.

3
Publishing Ngugi: The Challenge, the Risk, and the Reward

The history of Ngugi as a published writer goes back to the late 1950s when he was a student at Alliance High School in Kenya. His story, "Try Witchcraft," was published in the school magazine when he was in the second form, and another, "Voluntary Service Camp," appeared in the 1958 issue. Commercial success did not come until he was at Makerere University College in Kampala from 1959. While there, he wrote many stories, beginning with "The Fig Tree" ("Mugomo").

His first contact with a commercial publisher appears to have been in 1961, when his story, *The Black Messiah*, won first prize in a competition organized by the East African Literature Bureau. By this time, his potential as a writer of great promise had been recognized, and Heinemann was able to publish his second novel, *Weep Not Child*, in the African Writers Series in 1964, followed almost immediately by *The River Between*, a rewritten version of his earlier story, *The Black Messiah*. His more ambitious work, *A Grain of Wheat*, was published in the same series in 1967.

My own involvement with Ngugi started in the late 1960s when I was a literature student at the University of Nairobi and he was my tutor. Some time after I had secured my degree I joined Heinemann in Nairobi in 1972 as editor-in-training.

During this period, 1972–1986, I was responsible for receiving, evaluating, and selecting materials for publication in Heinemann's London-based African Writers Series, in close consultation with my colleagues in London and Ibadan. I was able to introduce new East African voices such as Meja Mwangi, Mwangi Ruheni, Sam Kahiga, Martha Mvungi, Mukotani Rugyendo, and Thomas Akare into the series while also publishing the more established writers, such as Okot

---

From *African Publishing Review* (1994).

p'Bitek, Taban lo Liyong, Joe de Graft, Rebeka Njau, and Micere Mugo. Not only did we publish many more new books by Ngugi over the same period but we also witnessed a transformation in the author-publisher relationship that had existed between Ngugi, Heinemann London, and Heinemann Kenya, and finally the transformation of Heinemann Kenya itself into an independent African imprint with the new name, East African Educational Publishers. *Petals of Blood* was the last of Ngugi's novels to be published by Heinemann in London in 1977. Even then, I insisted on a copublication arrangement and was able to fly a few hundred copies into Nairobi so that the title was launched there in July 1977 in the presence of Heinemann representatives from London and Ibadan. I shall return to the author-publisher relationship later as it forms the crux of this paper.

Ngugi, who was then chairman of the Department of Literature at the University of Nairobi, was constantly reminding me of the need to "localize" my publishing program so as to better fulfill the needs of the new curriculum. In response, I commissioned the first ever textbook of oral literature, which became an instant bestseller when it came out in 1982. It remains one of our most successful titles. In addition, I started a series of oral literature studies in Kenya's major languages. Although the running text was in English, the oral texts themselves were rendered in the original language, with English translations alongside. I have, to date, published the oral literatures of the Gikuyu, Maasai, and Kalenjin, with those of the Dholuo and Miji-Kenda in process.

A number of supplementary books, useful for the learning and teaching of oral literature, have also been published. Sales of these books were slow at first but they have now established themselves as standard reference books in schools, colleges, and universities. In addition, other publishers have followed our lead, and oral literature is now a popular publishing subject area.

If we accept that our literatures are to be found from among our own communities, in what language(s) must we express them? How should we share them among ourselves? Although it was agreed that the English language was vital for international communication, it was felt strongly that our writers should write for our own people and that, if the rest of the world saw any merit in what we were producing, they could access that material through translation into their own languages. We felt that it was time to prepare our communities and awaken them to the reality that they were the creators of their own literature. It was during this period (1976) that Ngugi (with his namesake, Ngugi wa Mirii) wrote *Ngaahika Ndeenda*—with the full critical participation of the people of Kamiriithu, who were later to stage it at the Kamiriithu Community Centre before large audiences.

But publishing in African languages was quite another proposition. What orthographies would we use, since some communities had none and others were reacting against those prepared for them by missionaries and were busy compiling new ones? Who would buy these books, in view of the fact that the majority of mother-tongue speakers were poor peasants who lived below the breadline, and only a small percentage of whom had achieved literacy beyond the 3Rs? As a publisher, how was I going to promote and distribute these books, in view of the fact that the majority of readers would be people from the rural areas where the roads are nonexistent or impassable for most of the year? In the absence of newspapers, journals, and other promotional outlets in those languages, how was I going to advertise these books?

Ngugi and I agonized over these matters for long hours, him optimistic, me skeptical. In the end we began to realize the power of translation. Who ever remembers that *War and Peace* and *Anna Karenina* were written in Russian? What about other classics like *Dead Souls*, *The Idiot*, *The Cherry Orchard*, *The Caucasian Chalk Circle*, *Hedda Gabler*, *The Plague*, *God's Bits of Wood*, and all those many books that we so much enjoy reading in English? Ngugi regretted that he had enriched the English language and culture with his novels *Weep Not Child*, *The River Between*, *A Grain of Wheat*, and *Petals of Blood* without giving anything back to the community, culture, and language that had inspired them. He swore that he would never write any more novels in English, but would henceforth write in the Gikuyu language.

In the years 1977 to 1982—before and after Ngugi's detention, which was during the whole of 1978—we spent much time together. The University of Nairobi administration had refused to allow him to resume his teaching duties, so I gave him a desk at my office where he could do his writing. After many discussions together, we were able to rationalize our ideas as follows: every community, every nationality, has its own languages, its own codified body of knowledge, its own literature, music, drama, dance, etc. Every community must accept the duty to preserve its own heritage, and should not rely on anyone else to do this for it. Every community is a concentric circle, complete in itself, and the good from it will flow and get absorbed into a broader national circle, which will in turn flow into a regional or continental circle, with only the best reaching the global circle.

We saw translation as the facilitator of those concentric circles and imagined a world where the Dholuo would be able to access materials written in Gikuyu, and vice versa, and the Luhya and Miji-Kenda would be able to compare their literatures. In our plan, works that transcended the first circle would be translated into Kiswahili and finally into English for dissemination nationally, regionally, and internationally. If people from countries where English is not spoken, such as France, Germany, Russia, Japan, Scandinavia, etc. expressed interest in any of our works, we would grant them rights to translate that work into their own language, sourcing their translation, as far as possible, from the original language. In this way, Africa would be exposing only the best of its creative output to the rest of the world.

I decided to start with children's books in mother tongues, and Ngugi himself volunteered to write the first three. I commissioned more children's books from the nation's leading writers—among them David Maillu, Francis Imbuga, Asenath Odaga, and Grace Ogot—and had published six new titles within a couple of years. In all sincerity, and in spite of the enthusiasm displayed by all my writers, I have to admit that these books did not do well and, to date, none of them has been reprinted. I was compelled to skip our second circle—that is, issuing them in Kiswahili translation, and commissioned English translations with some good results. International rights have been sold in only a few, including Ngugi's own.

Publishing Ngugi is a pleasurable and enriching experience. My direct publishing association with him dates back to 1975/76, when we worked together on *Petals of Blood*. Contrary to popular belief among academics and other creative writers who think we automatically accept Ngugi's books for publication, the script of *Petals*, then under the working titles "Wrestling with God" or "Wrestlers with God," was sent out for readers' reports in the normal way. I personally gave it an in-depth house report. Although all the reports recommended publication, they raised serious issues about the timing, movement, and content of the story, they noted constant repetition, felt that certain scenes had been contrived to achieve certain desired effects, and decried the predictability or inevitability of the storyline.

Ngugi took all these criticisms seriously and with great humility. He retrieved the script and reworked it for a long time, constantly coming back to seek clarification about some of our readers' criticisms. He listened to, even solicited, every comment, however casual, from my editors and other friends to whom he had given the script at his own initiative. To demonstrate how responsive Ngugi is to criticism and how he uses it constructively, I once made a casual observation to the effect that Wanja's *matatu* journey from Nairobi to Ilmorog, which was then identifiably Limuru, was too long and packed with too many incidents. I made a similar criticism of the delegation of workers and peasants from Ilmorog to Nairobi to meet their "lost" MP, which I again felt was overstretched and loaded with content that seemed to come out of Ngugi's mouth rather than that of his characters.

He responded to these criticisms by leaving all the incidents intact but "moving" Ilmorog so that it was now much further away from Nairobi, and its new description had changed from the lush green of Limuru to a drier place resembling Nyandarua, Kinangop, or Lari, or somewhere deeper into the Rift Valley. As for Wanja and her *matatu* journey, he seems to have edited it out of the novel altogether, later to reuse it in a much more integrated and creative manner in the next work, *Devil on the Cross*, where Wanja becomes Wariinga. Quite frankly, I cannot tell you which edition of *Petals of Blood* is in print, having read several versions of that novel both in manuscript and in proof!

I eventually came to accept Ngugi as being a little fastidious in his writing style, and I now know that, unless you stop him, he can go on rewriting a novel without stopping, responding to his critics, not by following their laid-down recommendations but by adopting a new approach that somehow takes care of their criticisms. The same story applies to proofs, which Ngugi will continue to change beyond his normal allocation, so that the publisher is forced to incur heavy correction costs. But the final product is usually a gem, giving great satisfaction to the editor and, I hope, to Ngugi himself. Ngugi treats his publisher as an equal partner in his creative process, and cooperates fully in carrying out the publisher's assignments and meets his deadlines promptly. I have never seen Ngugi lose his temper during our long publishing association. When we disagreed completely over the introduction to *The Trial of Dedan Kimathi*, which he had coauthored with Micere Mugo, he amicably asked us to rewrite it to what we wanted it to be, and ended the meeting.

My experience with the Gikuyu books was different, although equally enriching. It started with *Ngaahika Ndeenda*, a community-based effort in writing and producing a play. When he handed me the final script, Ngugi informed me that it had undergone a lot of fine-tuning by members of the cast and that he doubted if we needed to do any more work on it.

Beginning with *Ngaahika*, I established a pattern that was to repeat itself in the assessment of all works submitted by Ngugi in Gikuyu. Being a non-Gikuyu speaker myself, I had to find ways of overcoming my linguistic handicap before I could feel confident enough to offer his works for acceptance to our editorial board. The fact that we had no Gikuyu-speaking editor on our staff at that time meant that I could not benefit from an in-house assessment. We devised a strategy that was able to satisfy me as well as Ngugi and all those writers who participated in our "return of mother tongue" program.

Firstly, Ngugi would describe the plot in as much detail as possible, inviting comments from me at each stage. I would then give him the go-ahead to proceed with the writing. When the final script was ready, we would go through it together, page by page, with Ngugi explaining the story in meticulous detail. Once satisfied, I would submit the script to one or two Gikuyu readers for reports, and offer it for acceptance if the reports were positive, which they usually were.

Ngugi was determined that the Gikuyu editions of his books should be of the same production quality as their English counterparts, to forestall any thoughts that local-language publications were inferior or second-rate. For this reason, we were compelled to import new fonts for our typesetter, to enable him to do justice to the Gikuyu alphabet. We had to use the best designers and illustrators available, for his books. Once our designer produced a cover for *Caitani Mutharaba-ini*. It depicted a Mau Mau warrior stepping on a dead White soldier and with his AK47 rifle held high up in victory. Ngugi admired this cover for a long time and finally, in his modesty, declared it "too strong" for *Caitani*. He asked me to keep that cover safely, for he would write a new novel specifically for it. That novel was *Matigari*.

Ngugi is one of the few writers who believe that publishers are honest and decent people. He usually doesn't haggle over the terms that I propose to him. He will accept the percentage royalty proposed and the advance offered and might even agree to forego some benefit in order to "get the book started." Unlike other writers I know, he doesn't complain and fret that he has been to so and so bookshop and has not seen copies of his books, although he will from time to time suggest ideas as to how we might promote and distribute our books better. Again, unlike other writers, he does not go behind our back to visit the warehouse to check the bin cards or visit our accounts department to inspect the records to ensure that we are not holding back any royalties. He has absolute faith in people and their good intentions.

A real challenge as Ngugi's publisher was how I was going to distribute his books internationally, in the way that he was used to at Heinemann. I had already had some experience with *Petals of Blood*, published in London, but for which I had asked Heinemann to grant me East African rights in view of the role I had played in "developing" it with Ngugi. Secondly, when Heinemann declined to copublish Ngugi and Micere's *The Trial of Dedan Kimathi* with us, arguing that the African Writers Series was not for single collections of plays but for anthologies, I decided to publish the play in Nairobi.

Ngugi and Micere had written this play in anger because they were appalled by the manner in which Kenneth Watene had depicted Kimathi in his play, then just published and entitled *Dedan Kimathi*, and wanted a quick answer from us. Heinemann soon realized their mistake and eventually purchased rights from me to sell the play outside East Africa. I decided that as I did not have the marketing and distribution reach, I was going to sell rights, including translation rights, as widely as possible.

The African Writers Series was the automatic choice for English-language rights, and in the case of *Matigari*, for example, I was successful in selling French, Dutch, German, Danish, Swedish, American, and Japanese rights with assistance from Heinemann U.K. It is my belief and conviction that the books I have published with Ngugi are as well marketed and distributed as were his books when he was published by Heinemann in London.

There have been many threats, direct or indirect, that I or my company has suffered because of the association with Ngugi. Ngugi's books and other textbooks have been removed from official government reading lists; there have been other forms of censorship and harassment and the constant threat of litigation from members of the public who have felt libeled by Ngugi in his writings. Thankfully, none of these claimants have felt able to pursue their cases in a court of law. It is not for me to tell you how Ngugi himself has suffered, but it has obviously been on a much larger scale; and it is that suffering that still keeps him in exile today.

In spite of the problems I have been through, my association with Ngugi has been very rewarding, both intellectually and commercially. First and foremost, I must admit that my linkage with Heinemann's African Writers Series, and with Ngugi in particular, has played an important part in establishing and enhancing my reputation and that of East African Educational Publishers as the leading fiction publisher in the region, if not in the entire continent. My fiction list consists of drama, poetry, plays, novels, and oral literature works in mother tongue, Kiswahili, and English, not to mention children's books, all numbering 109 titles at present.

Further, there is not a single Ngugi book I have published (except the children's books in Gikuyu) that has not been an instant bestseller. *Ngaahika Ndeenda* and *Caitani Mutharaba-ini* went through three printings within the first year of publication, and their Kiswahili and English translations have performed equally well. I recently released an English translation of *Matigari* and it is performing well and will most likely go to a second printing this year. The original edition of *Matigari* remains in limbo, as we have not yet ascertained if we would be breaking the law by reissuing it. The essays, *Writers in Politics* and *Decolonising the Mind*, are in great demand, especially in our academic institutions, and are regularly reprinted; and *Moving the Centre*, only recently released, promises to be similarly successful. Rights have been acquired from Heinemann London on the earlier novels, and these, too, are published in Nairobi and continue to do well. Ngugi's long absence from Kenya, and the propaganda campaign that has been waged against him and his writings, has certainly affected the momentum of the sales of his books; but, excepting *Matigari*, all of them are in print and are not officially banned as is sometimes claimed in other circles.

What I have valued most is my intellectual association with Ngugi. He is a lot more committed, more serious, and more idealistic and ideologically inclined than I am, but we share the same philosophical and temperamental worldview. It is Ngugi's advice and the resultant exchange of views that encouraged me to give priority to oral literature in my publishing programs. It is Ngugi's conviction and my own willingness to experiment with some of his ideas that made me venture into publishing in African languages. Had Ngugi continued to live in Kenya, write more books in this line, and encourage his colleagues to support this venture, the program would have succeeded. In spite of my present setbacks in publishing in this area, I am waiting for the day when he will return home so that we can continue from where I stopped. In conclusion, although my association with Heinemann gave me a lot of international exposure, much of this has been sustained by the fact that I am the publisher of one of Africa's greatest and certainly its most controversial avant-garde writer, Ngugi wa Thiong'o. In selling rights of his books, I have had to interact with international publishers from all over the world: Japan, Russia, Germany, France, Scandinavia, the United States, and some African countries such as Zimbabwe and South Africa. At home, I enjoy quiet respect from serious-minded Kenyans who acknowledge the courageousness of keeping Ngugi's books in print under very difficult circumstances. The strong messages contained in his writings are much appreciated locally, even though this appreciation hardly finds public expression nowadays.

Chapter 4

An Autonomous African Publishing House: A Model

An autonomous institution is one that is responsible to itself, and exercises complete freedom in the control of its policies, finances, and management. An autonomous indigenous African publishing house must therefore be one owned and controlled by Africans themselves, either as individuals, or as a group, or working through an independent institution; and must itself be situated in Africa.

The majority of publishing houses in Africa are not autonomous. These include the most dominant category, namely the African branches of transnational publishing corporations controlled from outside the continent, and some state publishing houses that directly or indirectly fall under control of government.

At different locations and times, Africans have attempted to set up autonomous publishing houses with varying degrees of success. Many failed to become viable, in a commercial sense, and have collapsed. And a few have survived for some time—without, however, assuming the permanence or commercial resilience of their transnational competitors.

The main purpose of this study is to construct a model of a viable, autonomous, indigenous African publishing house, where viability also is seen to entail longevity and permanence. This model hopefully will assist those publishers already in business and those planning to set up business. But—also important—the model visualizes authentic and long-term African participation in the future of publishing in Africa.

The model itself is not based on any one existing house, but I have obviously drawn on the experiences of several publishing houses over the last ten years, some of which, sadly, are no longer in business.

From *Development Dialogue* (1984).

Our model publishing house should pursue the following aims and objectives:

- satisfy, at all levels, the country's educational needs;
- through its publications help in the popularization, dissemination, and preservation of the cultures and languages of the peoples of the country;
- be active in the production of children's books and adult literacy materials;
- contribute toward the entertainment needs of the country through, for example, works of fiction;
- guard its independence and not succumb to external political, financial, and ideological pressures;
- endeavor to reach the widest possible market within the country, in other African countries, and the rest of the world; and
- endeavor to be viable and profit making.

The model will work better in countries where a conducive publishing environment exists or can be established. Below are some of the conditions that must be satisfied, at least in part, before the model can be tested.

Entrepreneurship: publishing is a business and, like any other business, it needs an entrepreneur. The entrepreneur could be the publisher him- or herself or somebody who understands publishing and is, above all, committed to it, and is *not* just using it as a stepping stone to bigger things, such as politics, manufacturing, etc. The entrepreneur should not look at publishing as a seasonal or part-time occupation, and above all, must be able to put the money together either through his or her own resources or by means of a bank loan.

Finance: publishing requires considerable funding up front. In addition to the usual recurrent overhead expenses, our publisher will need money to initiate and develop projects. A title can take up to nine months (in some cases as long as two years) from initiation to finished copies. They must therefore have sufficient funds to see them through the initial period when expenditure will exceed income. I recommend a minimum capital of U.S.$250,000 for the entrepreneur wishing to set up a publishing house.

Personnel: our publishing house must be manned by fully trained and experienced personnel, skilled in all aspects of book work, and with qualifications comparable to those employed by foreign-based publishing houses. The publisher should not allow any compromising of standards and professionalism just because the operation is indigenous.

Superstructure and infrastructure: our publisher's work will be easier if an adequate superstructure and infrastructure exist, and in places where these do not exist, every effort must be made to create them. The term superstructure is used here to refer to authors, readers, designers, artists, and all those upon whom a publisher draws to get books developed. By infrastructure, I refer to a whole host of auxiliary industries and outlets such as paper manufacturers, film and plate-makers, printers, booksellers, etc.

THE MODEL ITSELF
First Principles

Offices: choose modest offices in modest surroundings. Remember that in Africa, publishing is still a small business.

Staff: you can open business with a minimum of five staff members—yourself, a secretary, an editor, a salesperson, and an office helper.

Publishing program: your publishing program must be carefully planned. It is important to achieve a balanced mix of short-term, midterm, and long-term projects. I would recommend starting with short-term projects, by which I mean low-risk books that attract modest investment and are faster to produce. Examples are revision books, students' guides, examination crammers, etc.

Recommended subject areas: in respect to the aims and objectives stated above, you need to identify priority publishing areas that are comparatively less risky. I recommend starting with books at the primary and secondary school level. First produce the supplementary books mentioned above, and then, as your publishing expands, you can venture into longer-term investment projects such as textbooks. These require more money up front, have a longer gestation period and carry greater risks, but they produce attractive profits when you break through.

Launching into the market: launch into the market with at least five titles (preferably ten) so as to make an impact, establish credibility, create a favorable image, and make your sales staff cost-effective.

Plan your growth: do not be overambitious by going for every book and every author that come your way. There may be some virtue in being the largest or the fastest-growing publisher but it also has its shocks, strains, and stresses. Once you have a work force of 30 to 40 people and are publishing 30 to 40 titles a year, and have a turnover of around U.S.$2 million, I would advise you to slow down, consolidate your business, and increase its profitability to 15 percent or more, before making plans for further expansion.

Distribution: I would recommend that in the early stages of your business, you distribute your books through an agent or agents, so that you can devote more time to the two most important departments in a publishing house: editorial and sales. Only when commission to the distribution agent(s) has fallen to 10 percent of turnover or below, should you consider setting up your own distribution department or company.

Some Hard and Fast Rules

Readers fees: you will need to develop a corpus of readers in key areas to assess the manuscripts you receive, and to advise you on your various projects. Avoid giving out each and every manuscript you receive to readers, and do not purchase manuscripts outright, however good you may think they are. Keep your readers fees at very modest levels—that is, pay a token of appreciation rather than a commercial fee. An average of U.S.$30 per manuscript is recommended.

Author's advance: this should be kept fairly modest, and should be paid only when a larger part of the manuscript is complete. Avoid paying out money on commission, and do not offer an advance for every book or every idea you come across.

Contracts: these should be prepared and signed only when the complete manuscript has been delivered. Negotiate royalty terms of around 10 percent of published price or 12.5 percent of receipts, or thereabouts. Total advance payable should be in the region of one-third of the anticipated total royalty earnings for the first printing, and should certainly not exceed 50 percent. High royalty percentages, though attractive on paper, are counterproductive to both the publisher and the author.

Production: you should ensure that books are produced as fast as possible, preferably within 12 months (latest) from delivery of the complete manuscript. Shop around for the best printing prices in the market, and strive to obtain at least 60 to 90 days credit from the printer. You should avoid the temptation of doing your own typesetting or buying your own paper, etc., but if you do have to do it, wait until much later when you are more established and more profitable.

Print runs: avoid the temptation of printing too many copies in order to get a good unit price. In these days of tight money controls, high interest rates and inflation, I recommend printing only the number of copies you can sell within 12 months.

Pricing: you should price your books in such a way that you achieve a margin of well over 50 percent—55 percent is recommended. Avoid soliciting subsidies to overcome your pricing problems.

Credit terms to booksellers and other retailers: I suggest 25 percent discount on schoolbooks and 35 percent on general books and a maximum credit period of 60 to 90 days. If there are not enough bookshops and other distribution outlets in your territory, I personally recommend supplying direct to institutions (for cash) in areas where bookshops do not exist, or through other distribution channels such as grocery stores, etc. I would not recommend sending books out on consignment as this could lead to much loss and wastage. Very strict credit control must be maintained, and supplies to those customers who do not pay on time should be stopped at once.

Overhead: make sure that these costs are contained to within 35 percent of revenue or less. You should be prepared to take drastic measures, such as cutting down on staff or moving to smaller premises, in order to maintain your overhead at this level.

Cash flow: in the initial stages your expenditure will exceed revenue, for reasons inherent in the previous points. But you should aim to reserve this trend in the first 2 to 3 years. After that you should ensure that your cash flow is positive, rather than negative, at all times. Take immediate remedial action, such as cutting down on new projects or reducing print runs, in addition to the suggestions given above (see discussion of overhead), if you find yourself in a negative cash flow situation.

Net profit: aim at a profit before tax upwards of 15 percent.
Return on capital: aim at a return on capital upwards of 25 percent.

Success or failure will depend largely on management capability. Careful planning, proper decision making, a knack for knowing what will sell, judicious employment of funds, close supervision, and strict adherence to the controls mentioned above are essential. Above all, you must remain committed to publishing and determined to make a success of it.

Corporate Image

Publishing is a vital and high-profile industry. You should make it a priority to develop a proper modus operandi and a favorable cooperate image.

Staff: everything must be done to recruit, train, and retain staff of integrity on terms comparable to those offered by foreign publishers and to motivate them so that they are totally committed and reflect a favorable image for the company at all times.

Government: you will need to establish a good working relationship with government. Indeed, you will undoubtedly discover that most people in government know little or nothing about publishing. It will be your duty to educate them about your role as a person of business and an educator. All transactions with government must be at arm's length, and you should steer clear of any corrupt practices. You must seek government protection from unfair competition but should not expect any favors just because you are indigenous.

Public: you will build a good public image for yourself if you publish good books in good time, pay authors' royalties and answer letters promptly, and speed up assessments of manuscripts to within 8 to 12 weeks of submission. Constant mailings, catalogs, and stocklists (which must be updated every year) will keep the reading public continually aware of what you are doing.

Press: as the public is more likely to hear about you and your books in the press than any other way, you need to cement your relationships with newspapers and magazines. It is too expensive to advertise effectively in papers but do maintain a good personal relationship by giving out review copies, press releases, feature articles, etc., and take advantage of whatever features on publishing they themselves set up.

Other publishers: although you are competing for the same market, you would be well advised to maintain a good working relationship with your colleagues in the industry, regardless of whether they work for local or foreign firms. There has been undue emphasis on competition between local and foreign publishers. I believe there is much scope for both kinds of publisher, and room for a mutually beneficial relationship at this stage of development in Africa's publishing industry. Both are involved in developing books and courses in largely unexplored fields and are encountering similar problems, and so can benefit from each other's experiences. Join the publishers association where it exists, and try to set one up if it does not exist. It will be your mouthpiece in dealing with government and public. Support other book-related industries. Do not import anything you can obtain locally. There are cases of publishers who print abroad when they have a viable printing industry at home, or import paper instead of supporting their own paper mill. Support the booksellers as much as possible, while seeking alternative ways of widening the book distribution network in your territory.

International agencies: make yourself known and heard outside your own territory. Pursue joint publication deals with international publishers. Establish links with international agencies such as CREPLA,

UNESCO, IPA, etc., and make them aware of your activities. Supply information promptly to such institutions as may be required from time to time. If you can afford it, go to book fairs (Frankfurt, Bologna, Ife, Zimbabwe, etc.) and display your publications there. You may be surprised to discover that international publishers want to buy rights on some of your titles. Also look out for opportunities to buy rights from international publishers for titles that might have potential in your market. Some may approach you to represent them, or distribute their books in your territory. If their list complements your own, you might find them a source of additional revenue, but always remember that you are a publisher in your own right and not somebody else's distributor.

The following obstacles may well occur:

Manpower: there are few people in Africa with the relevant skills in book production. Trained editors, book designers, and illustrators are rare and few training facilities exist. The small number of people with the necessary training have been trained by and work for the transnationals.

Finance: publishing is a small, risky, and capital-intensive venture. For these reasons, it does not always receive priority from banks and other money-lending institutions when it comes to borrowing. The long gestation period before a manuscript becomes a book and before the book can become profitable calls for a long-term loan with a two- or three-year grace period, a prospect that would-be financiers are usually reluctant to accept.

Competition: indigenous publishers find themselves up against competition from the more established transnational publishing firms, some of which operate branches in Africa and have a strong grip on the market. African governments should protect and strengthen African publishing houses and at the same time assist their nationals to gain control of the African branches of the transnationals operating in their territory.

In addition to the above, our African publisher will face certain problems encountered by all other publishers in the continent. These include:

Ignorance: most people, including civil servants and politicians in high positions, do not understand what publishing is about. They are therefore less sympathetic to publishers' problems, and less appreciative of their important role in national development.

Illiteracy: approximately 65 percent of the continent is illiterate, and 20 percent have a fairly basic education, with the ever-present danger of lapsing back into illiteracy. The publisher in Africa publishes for only about 20 percent of the population.

Language: Africa is reported to have well over 1,200 languages in use. Out of these only about 600 have been transcribed. This means that many Africans do not have access to materials written in their own languages. Moreover, speakers of most of the languages already transcribed, including those brought by colonialism, constitute a minority in any one African country. Therefore, a decision to publish in any language, be it local or foreign, in most cases cuts out the majority of potential readers in that country.

Reading habits: a reading culture has not yet fully developed in Africa. Few people voluntarily read books, and most stop reading at the end of their formal education. The potential market is thus further depressed.

Censorship: some publishers in Africa are victims of state censorship and others censor themselves by not publishing books that ought to be published because of fear of falling afoul of the government in power.

Poverty: most people are struggling for the bare necessities of life, and regard books as an unnecessary luxury.

SOME CONCLUDING REMARKS

In this paper, emphasis has been given to autonomy from foreign control and influence. It must, however, be recognized that our model publisher will not be free to do whatever he likes; his board, his shareholders, and financiers will be there to ensure that his freedom is exercised within limits.

It must also be stressed that the model presented here is not the only way to successfully launch onto the African publishing scene. It is offered not as gospel, but as one possible way of approaching it.

The model was prepared as a working document and can, therefore, be modified in places or even changed to suit existing situations in the country where it may be tested. Whatever its limitations, it will have achieved its purpose if it stimulates further thoughts and actions toward a strategy for the development of autonomous publishing houses in Africa.

5

International Copyright and Africa: The Unequal Exchange

The recently concluded rights indaba,[1] which coincided with the 1994 Zimbabwe International Book Fair in Harare, brought into the spotlight the thorny issue of African and international copyright. The conference had been organized originally as a means of promoting book trade among African states. In the end, it turned out to be a training session, with European publishers educating their African colleagues on how best to sell rights in international markets. In spite of reports to the contrary, it is unlikely that the conference achieved its prime objective of increasing trade in rights or indeed the original one of increasing cross-border trade among the African publishers themselves. The speakers from the North advised African publishers that, in order to make their rights offers more attractive to foreign buyers, they should surrender as much territory as possible. For example, a Zimbabwe publisher should retain only Zimbabwe, and release the rest of the market to the foreign buyer. They were advised not to insist on too high a royalty—7 percent was recommended as acceptable—and to curb their tendency to ask for too high an advance, because African books are difficult to sell in the North. Above all, they were urged to improve on the quality and presentation of their products and improve their promotion and marketing strategies before, during, and after publication of their books. Other somewhat patronizing bits of advice were offered, and one got the impression that African publishers were now being called upon to abandon their principal aim of serving their own markets and concentrate on satisfying the needs of foreign rights buyers.

The printed word still remains the easiest, cheapest, and most versatile method of communicating and distributing knowledge. The book, in particular, is handy, presentable, easy to store, and readily

From P. G. Altbach, ed., *Copyright and Development* (1995).

adaptable to dissemination, retrieval, and transfer of knowledge, in whole or in part. With widespread use of radio and television, coupled with recent advances in the information industry such as video, reprography, computer networking, and other innovations facilitating fast transfer of information such as fax, electronic mail, the Internet, etc., it was feared that the role of the book and printing technology in general, would decline. This may be the case in some countries but, on the whole, it would appear that the book has not only stood its ground but has again come in handy in the use, application, and promotion of these new technologies. Today, the position of the book remains central to the dissemination of knowledge and that reality is unlikely to change in the foreseeable future, especially in Africa. In addition, although it is probably the slowest, most "primitive," and most demanding method of transferring knowledge, the book remains the most effective, in spite of the fact that it does not carry any compensating features.[2]

In this essay, we shall not discuss international copyright per se, or whether or not it serves the interests of justice and equity. We shall merely observe that trade in copyright makes sense only when applied to two equal or almost equal partners, who buy as much as they sell from each other. If one has little or nothing to sell, one administers copyright only in the interests of those who have it. Yet it has to be accepted that international copyright is necessary, even inevitable, if intellectual property is to be protected, its distribution controlled, and those responsible for its creation rewarded and acknowledged for their work. This must be accepted as crucial in shaping and improving the quality of life on a more permanent and long-lasting basis. We shall argue that unless international copyright is administered in a manner that facilitates the sharing of the world's intellectual property and not as a tool of capitalistic selfishness and protectionism, the developing world should regard it with suspicion and should not subscribe to it without certain safeguards and assurances. It is not accidental that some of the world's largest book producers today, such as the former Soviet Union, do not yet subscribe to international copyright. Additionally, today's major book giants, among them the United States, Japan, and China, did not agree to the Berne Convention and its various protocols until they had developed strong national book industries of their own. What promise, then, does international copyright hold out for Africa, given the fact that 34 out of its 54 countries are members of the Berne

Convention?[3] Before we attempt to answer this question, let us take a survey of the available literature on this subject to see if it can illuminate our discussion.

THE LITERATURE ON COPYRIGHT

Most of the literature available on the market, some of which is listed in the bibliography at the end of this essay, does not question or critically examine international copyright, and its positive or negative effects on the world knowledge industry. It merely sets out to explain the law and how it is being enforced, and with what results. A plethora of publications contain advice on how to draw up publishing agreements to cover the variety of rights subsisting in a publication, as seen largely from the point of view of the publisher in the North.

The International Publishers Association, the Scientific Technical Medical Publishers Association, the World Intellectual Property Organization (WIPO), the International Federation of Reproduction Rights Organizations (IFRRO), the mushrooming national reproduction rights organizations (RROs), and national publishing associations in the North, contain up-to-date information on copyright: which countries have signed and which are about to sign the various conventions and protocols governing its use—from Florence, the Universal Copyright Convention (UCC), to Berne, culminating in their Paris accords, and all the other protocols that have followed. The activities of the various watchdog institutions policing copyright receive constant coverage, as do the new structures being set up especially in the developing world, for this purpose. The manner and extent of copyright infringement, where and when, are constantly highlighted, complete with damages that have been paid or imposed, and what new devices are being developed to deal with piracy and what these organizations are doing to cope with the ever-increasing list of threats brought about by the new technologies. Needless to add, this information is essentially for the benefit and the interest of the North, and Africa receives a mention only when a new African country signs or ratifies these agreements. Philip Altbach's *The Knowledge Context: Comparative Perspectives on the Distribution of Knowledge*[4] is one book that adopts an analytical and critical approach similar to the one posited in this essay.

AIMS

This essay seeks to bring out and comment upon the social and economic impact of international copyright as it affects the developing world today, to assess the effects of this on the distribution of knowledge. Moreover, it is crucial to define how the present copyright relationship makes possible or hinders the sharing and transfer of knowledge between the North and the South. More specifically, an attempt is made to examine the relevance or irrelevance of international copyright in so far as the present realities of publishing practice in Africa are concerned—what problems or constraints prevent it from exploiting these provisions in order to bring about the free flow of information from North to South, and vice versa. We shall look briefly at the future of the printed word in a rapidly changing world and extrapolate on the extent to which international copyright can continue to maintain the central and strategic role in the world knowledge industry today and whether it has the capacity, the will, and resources to "tame" and control the ever-mushrooming new technologies that are constantly threatening its administration. Finally, while subscribing to the view that international copyright is necessary, we shall conclude by making a few proposals aimed at "humanizing" it in order to make it more responsive to the needs and knowledge requirements of the developing world in general, and Africa in particular.

THE REALITY: AFRICA'S OUTPUT

The reality in Africa, as in the rest of the world today, is that more and more countries are promulgating laws governing national copyright and signing and/or ratifying international copyright treaties, and in some countries enforcement is being incorporated into national statutes. Some countries have set up or are in the process of setting up RROs to protect copyright and guard against piracy, not only in the area of publishing but also in such other areas as music performance, reprography, and public library rights. International agencies, especially WIPO and IFRRO, are busy providing technical and financial assistance in the drafting, administration, and enforcement of these laws, offering training where it is needed.

The success of these lobbies can be seen in the fact that to date, according to available data, 106 countries, including China, India, Taiwan, and Germany, have become members of the Berne Convention. The United States, after years of membership only in the UCC, has also joined Berne. Others, such as Russia and North and South Korea, are reported to be positively responding to pressure to join. Out of the 106 members mentioned above, 34 are from Africa and constitute nearly one-third of the total membership of the Berne Convention,[5] leaving only 24 of the remaining African states out but likely to join in the near future. The reasons why African countries have signed these conventions are difficult to understand. The 1993 UNESCO *Statistical Year Book*[6] shows that although Africa has 12 percent of the world's population, it produces only 1.2 percent of its books, and that this percentage is declining. Comparatively, Europe produces 53 percent of the world's books, compared to Asia (27 percent) and North American (13 percent). The situation is no different with newspapers, magazines, journals, and other reading materials, and they have already taken a commanding lead in the development of the new technologies referred to above. In his book, Altbach observes that 80 percent of the world's knowledge industries are based in the North and their output is copyrighted there. This means that African countries have signed these protocols, not to protect their own knowledge industries, but to ensure that their people do not use or abuse other peoples' rights.

There seems to be little or no difference in the publishing fortunes or destiny of those countries who have signed copyright agreements, and those who have not. For example, Tanzania was not a signatory until very recently, yet its publishing industry remains one of the least developed in Africa. Neighboring Kenya has a fairly well-developed industry, yet this cannot be attributed to the fact that it was one of the early signatories to these conventions. Moreover, a lack of publishing capacity, resources, and training makes it difficult to say whether it is Africa's adherence to international copyright or its lack of capacity that has prevented it from engaging in unlawful reprinting, photocopying, and pirating of copyrightable materials. We do not know of any African state or publisher who has willfully contravened international copyright as was the case in Asia, especially between the 1950s and the 1980s, although we are aware that there has been pirating of books from Asia to West Africa, especially Nigeria.[7]

A closer look at the list of the other states that belong to the Berne

Convention shows that these are countries with highly developed publishing industries with a major interest to protect. As we have already observed, major book powers such as the United States, Japan, India, and China delayed signing and ratifying these conventions until they had something to offer the world. One can only assume that African countries have chosen to sign because they believe this will facilitate the flow of knowledge from the North to their own countries. What compensation or reparation can Africa get from the North for this bold act of chivalry? Indeed, if this is so, we shall argue that this view still makes sense only in the short run and only if there is cooperation from rights holders in the North, but the reality of the situation is that these rights holders do not appear keen to extend printing licenses to African publishers. Instead, they are using copyright as a weapon to maintain the dependency relations that currently exist. The African signatories have arrogated themselves the role of collecting copyright fees from their own people and remitting these to the owners in the North.

This has serious repercussions for the cost of education, and for the future of education industries in Africa. When Africa finally gets to Professor Minowa's "takeoff" point[8]—when the necessary economic, production, and distribution infrastructures will be in place and the market sufficiently developed to permit proper commercial publishing to emerge—this is when the magnanimous gesture of the majority of its member states will catch up with this reality. It will find that its hands are tied, and that is when it will replace Asia as the battleground for piracy and other copyright infringement battles presently raging in the rest of the world. For now, lack of capacity and throughput resulting primarily from poverty renders the issue of which countries are signatories and which are not somewhat academic.

AFRICA HAS LITTLE TO OFFER . . .

Even if copyright laws were to be administered equitably, and in Africa's best interest, Africa would find that it has little or nothing to sell to the outside world. Its textbooks, which constitute nearly 90 percent of its total output, can hardly travel within national boundaries, let alone outside Africa. As a matter of fact, a large proportion of these textbooks are published by European publishers or their African branches so that, essentially, the copyright in these works is held by publishers in the North.

The remaining 10 percent of Africa's book output is made up of liturgical materials, children's books, fiction, academic books, and gray literature. The liturgical materials include the standard Bible, hymn books, and Bible stories—mainly in African languages, published by mission presses, controlled by the centers of world religions, most of them based in the North. Its children's books are few and not produced to a quality level that can attract foreign interest. Inadequate production expertise and lack of investment finance, and imprudent minimization of risk have led to poor production and marketing and distribution strategies, and encouraged excessive reliance on textbook publishing, which enjoys a ready market. Academic books are few and are mostly published outside the continent anyway, as is most of the fiction.

Africa's leading fiction writers are published in the North, mostly in Britain, France, and the United States. The majority of them sprang into prominence in the 1950s and 1960s, when the African publishing industry was either in its nascent stage, or did not exist at all. They continue to be published in those centers partly because local African industries are not yet sufficiently developed to provide maximum exposure to their works, or because they are still bound by contractual obligations to their original publishers. Most publishers in the North have a clause in all their contracts that reads as follows: "The publishers shall have the first refusal of the author's next two works suitable for publication for the education market (and the author shall offer to the publishers for this purpose the same rights and territories as those covered by this agreement) on terms to be mutually agreed . . .," a Catch-22 clause that is self-perpetuating. If UNESCO's report that Africa produces 1.2 percent of the world's books is true, then it would appear that the continent controls only about 0.4 percent of the world's intellectual property, a sad reality for the 34 African countries that subscribe to the Berne Convention and constitute the largest bloc of members from any continent.

Take the issue of research, for example. Most African countries do not have the institutional structures, resources, or expertise to engage in research. Most of the research is undertaken by scholars from the North, whose findings are published and copyrighted in the North. It would be foolish to halt essential research for this reason. As we shall argue in the concluding section of this essay, the solution is to "humanize" international copyright, both in principle and practice, so that it does not remain a selfish tool in the hands of the rich North. One research area that reveals a glaring contradiction is African oral literatures and traditions that cannot be claimed to be the intellectual property of anybody in particular. Yet, as soon as this is researched into, and the material compiled and published by the researcher (most of them are from the North), it becomes his copyright, and no one can use it without permission. A few African countries have made certain exceptions about oral literatures and traditions in their national copyright laws, but it does not pay for them to behave like a dog in a manger, and research into these areas is in the interest of scholarship and must go on. Moreover, we should not, as we are doing, accuse publishers in the North of hoarding copyright when we ourselves are placing restrictions on our own intellectual property, for it can be said that oral literature is the vehicle for the exchange of information for about 75 percent of the entire population of Africa.

We have argued that in spite of having signed and ratified international copyright instruments, African publishers have little or nothing to offer in the facilitation of the free flow of knowledge between nations, one of the cardinal assumptions of international copyright. They are too poor and have little capacity and no experience in the buying and selling of rights. Their foreign counterparts frequently take advantage of them on the few occasions that they engage in such transactions, taking the whole territory when they buy and restricting them to their home ground when they sell. We have also argued that existing copyright watchdogs, whether policed by international agencies such as WIPO, IFRRO, or national RROs, are not focused toward preventing copyright infringement in African-published works, thus allowing publishers in the North to take advantage of this situation and to freely flout the very laws that they apply to safeguard their interests in the South. Further, we have argued that although the publishing situation in Africa is improving, the present trend is likely to continue for a while yet, as we do not yet foresee a situation in the near future whereby research in Africa will be controlled by African governments and scholars. We have cautioned that the area of oral literatures and traditions is particularly vulnerable, and although several African governments have declared that area to be in the public domain, the majority of scholars who carry out research in it continue to copyright their findings. We shall now see what the North has to offer, and we will be able to establish the extent to which international copyright is a facilitator or a hindrance in the knowledge transfer process between the North and the South.

THE NORTH HAS EVERYTHING TO OFFER, BUT . . .

As we have already noted, there is little publishing activity taking place in Africa. One way of speeding up the knowledge transfer process is for the publishers in the North to grant reprint licenses to their African counterparts to facilitate faster and cheaper production, and stimulate capacity building. However, experience over the last 30 years has shown that these publishers would rather set up local branches in Africa, or sell directly from the metropole than grant licenses. They are particularly reluctant to sublicense school textbooks even to those countries that have capacity to manufacture them locally. It cannot be argued that they make less profit when they sell rights since in cases where such rights are granted, they would normally insist on a maximum royalty of 20 percent (which goes into their books "below the line"), yet the majority do not net that kind of profit in their normal publishing operations. We can only surmise that the real reason is selfish and protectionist—they do not want to transfer capacity and the skills that go with its development.

We have also stated that international copyright protects the haves, not the have-nots, and is structured to serve the interests of those with something to protect. This was clearly demonstrated in a recent copyright case[9] in the High Court of Kenya, where a British multinational publisher sued a local Kenyan publisher for breach of copyright in a Kiswahili[10] novel that had not been reissued for eight years, but that had suddenly come into prominence by being prescribed for the local "O" level literature examination. In spite of the existence of a new contract signed between the local author and publisher, and while not disputing the fact that the book had been out of print for that period, the judge[11] ruled in favor of the British publisher, arguing that as the author had not repossessed his rights from the original publisher, expressly in writing, he had nothing to sell the Kenyan publisher. As the author had died in the meantime, it was not possible to have him in court to testify, but, even then, the judge did not listen to any witnesses and insisted that without a release letter from the British publisher, the local publisher and his author did not have a foot to stand on. This clearly demonstrates that international copyright is tilted toward the interests of metropolitan publishers, who use the letter of law to ensure that rights do not revert to their rightful owners even when they themselves are not in a position to fully exploit them. Other cases have been reported whereby European publishers maintain the minimum stock levels of works by African authors as stipulated in the author-publisher contract, refusing to release them for sale, so that, technically, the work remains in print and they retain copyright until another opportunity to exploit them arises. Unless a provision is made in international copyright conventions to discourage and even punish hoarding of copyright in these and other ways, publishers in the North will continue to use it to deny the developing world essential knowledge material vital to its development.

In the few exceptional cases where European publishers grant rights to their African counterparts, this is usually done on harsh and unfavorable terms. The license normally covers one printing only, specifying the print run, but with provision for the grantee to renegotiate a new reprint, which, if granted, is then covered by a fresh contract. The license restricts the territory to the country of the publisher's domicile, so that a Kenyan publisher granted such a license cannot sell his licensed books in neighboring "common" market territories such as Uganda and Tanzania. The royalty demanded is usually between 15 and 20 percent, and where foreign exchange permits, this payment is required to be paid up front on publication, and/or a sizable advance and offset fees are insisted upon in the contract license and must be paid before the license can come into force. Additionally, the African publisher is required to print in one of the preliminary pages of his edition words to the effect that "This reprint has been authorized by (name of publisher) for sale in (name of territory / country) only and not for export therefrom. . . ." Some British rights holders will even insist on having a say in the pricing of the licensed book, the printers to use, and the trade discounts to give to certain of their favored booksellers and distributors in the African publisher's territory.

Yet, in cases where the European publisher is buying rights from an African publisher, he is the one who determines the terms, as was so clearly described at the Harare indaba. The African publisher must retain only his own territory, and must offer the rest to the buyer. In addition, the buyer must be granted all subsidiary rights, including translation rights. The seller should ask for a royalty of 5 percent, certainly not more than 7 percent, and should request only a "nominal" advance, if any. If possible, the contract should not carry any time limitation, but if it does, a minimum of 5 years, renewable, was recommended. When the book is eventually published, often the foreign publisher does not acknowledge the original African publisher anywhere in the book, and will sometimes claim in his blurb and publicity material that the author is "a new discovery."

As we can see, rights holders in the North want to cling to their rights as tightly as possible, whether they are buying or selling, and if and when they decide to buy or sell, they prefer to maintain a North-South vertical axis that cannot facilitate intra-African trade, as each state or publisher is made to sign a separate contract with the foreign publisher on the same title in the same region. The African states themselves are already resigned to this manner of trading with their erstwhile colonial masters, and as books constitute an infinitesimal volume of the business that follows this pattern in Africa's international trade, they cannot be expected to see the urgency of addressing this problem or, for that matter, the dangers of acceding to existing international copyright conventions or promulgating their local copyright laws based on existing international models. The original intention of the Harare indaba was to promote intra-African trade horizontally, so that African countries can be encouraged to trade with each other, not only in finished books but in rights as well, so that an African market in books can be engendered and strengthened. You cannot eat your cake and still have it. By going about this noble objective in the way that it did, the indaba squandered a rare opportunity. It would have been more meaningful if African publishers had talked among themselves first and formed a pressure group to plead with foreign publishers to adopt a humane approach in their copyright administration policies, than to sit with them at the same table and be taught how to deal in rights—as if that was the only problem.

The international watchdog agencies that police copyright infringement are not geared toward protecting copyright in works originating from Africa. They are concerned more with guarding the interests of the North, whose publishers produce the majority of copyrightable materials. African publishers, themselves, with or without assistance from their own governments, do not have the capacity, knowhow, experience, or even the will to defend the little that they have. At the Harare conference, stories were told of foreign publishers who publish the works of African scholars without even notifying them or signing any form of agreement. A sharp exchange arose between one foreign agent who was busy negotiating rights with the estate of a dead writer whose book was, in fact, still in print with Tanzania Publishing House! We are ourselves aware that publishers in Germany, Italy, Japan, etc. continue to publish certain titles originally published by the now defunct East African Publishing House, even though that company has long been bankrupt, and some of the authors have transferred their rights to other local rights holders. Attempts to get those publishers to confirm or deny this have fallen on deaf ears, even when we have sought the assistance of their embassies in Nairobi. In some cases, we have been informed that the books have gone out of print, yet one sometimes spots copies of these licensed editions, usually in translation, on display at such fairs as Frankfurt and Bologna.

My company has dealt in the rights trade perhaps more than any other African publisher outside South Africa. We have nearly 100 licensed titles on our list, approximately 15 percent of our backlist and have had rights dealings in at least 50 of our locally originated titles. We have been subjected to some of the prejudices mentioned above, although we must admit that we have found American publishers more understanding and more sympathetic to our requests than their British counterparts, especially in their readiness to grant rights faster and on better terms. Admittedly, we have not dealt with the Americans on licensing their textbooks, as our business, to date, has been restricted mainly to African studies publications. The majority of licenses grant us the Kenya market only, but in a few exceptional cases we get Kenya, Uganda, and Tanzania, and sometimes even Africa. Only with James Currey Publishers,[12] in London, do we have copublication arrangements that enable each party to exploit the rights and market potential of each title to the full.

HUMANIZING INTERNATIONAL COPYRIGHT

Africa's publishing capacity is bound to increase in future, thanks to the interest that African governments, international donor agencies, and nongovernmental organizations (NGOs) are beginning to show in this sector. The activities of the African Publishers' Network (APNET), formed two years ago, are drawing sympathetic and active support even from NGOs and donor agencies on the North—including the World Bank, which has become a major player on the African book publishing scene. The Bank is currently revising its book procurement procedures with a view to encouraging more books and materials acquisition through local competitive bidding and direct contracting more than the international competitive bidding approach it has used in the past, which has tended to favor foreign suppliers and suppress local participation in the tendering process. Others are assisting in training, capitalizing, and strengthening the marketing and distribution structures, as well as encouraging the growth of local and regional publishers associations, and, of course, giving support to APNET itself.

At the same time, African governments are beginning to appreciate the need to liberalize and privatize the industry, delink it from the state, and generally create an even playing field, where quality and fair competition will be the hallmark. These efforts are likely to result in a more invigorated African publishing industry in the next decade or two, but they are unlikely to stem the negative impact of international copyright, now or then, unless attention is given to the recommendations that follow. We shall make these as simply, clearly, and as tentatively as possible and on the premises that, while fulfilling the original intentions of international copyright, they will help to facilitate maximum exploitation of the world's intellectual property to benefit all. The overriding assumptions behind the proposals, as explained above, include the need to develop and expand publishing capacity in the developing world through maximizing the transfer of knowledge from the rich to the book-poor countries. It is also assumed that a need exists to standardize the rules, written and unwritten, that currently guide collective copyright administration by rights holders as enforced by their national, regional, and international copyright monitoring agencies and reinforced by their governments. Finally, it is assumed that the collective administration of copyright should, first and foremost, be in the interest of knowledge, rather than for the advancement of trade, although we recognize the rights of writers and other creators to be rewarded for their creations. We shall first deal with what should or can be done now and conclude by making some suggestions for the future.

Author's contracts are drawn up by publishers in the North for their own authors and for those who seek reprint licenses from them. These contracts should be examined again and again to determine to what extent they conform to the letter and spirit of international copyright and national copyright laws. The rules governing their granting of licenses, or their refusal to grant such licenses, must be subjected to international scrutiny with a view to having them revised to incorporate the human factor, and all publishers should be prevented from directly refusing to grant reprint licenses on flimsy grounds or without giving reasons.

International copyright agencies such as WIPO, the International Publishers Copyright Council, Copyright Clearance Center in the United States, Copyright Licensing Agency in the United Kingdom, and other national RROs, working closely with publishers and governments of the developed world, should provide a two-way service in their copyright protection activities. As we have pointed out in this essay, publishers in the North continue to flout with impunity the same conventions that are protecting their interests in the South. As a demonstration of transparency and good faith, these agencies should recruit more Africans into their organizations to help tilt their policies and focus toward the developing world. Further, they or any others affiliated with them should devise a mechanism for releasing, on a regular basis, a list of out-of-print titles—with tips on which major titles are about to go out of print, and which ones are back in print. These lists should be widely publicized, especially in the South so that any publishers wishing to reissue some of these titles may make the necessary arrangements to do so. Finally, the foreign publishers who insist on being granted world rights by the African writers they contract and who then sell some of those rights to the United States or other rights buyers on the writers' behalf must do this with the full knowledge and consent of the writers. In most cases, the African writer has little knowledge and no control over such a sale, or any sale of subsidiary rights for that matter, so that when a book thus sold goes out of print in those subsidiary markets, the rights revert to the foreign publisher rather than to the author who is the rightful owner, and to add insult to injury, information about such transactions is not always conveyed to the writer, unless he makes a specific request for it. Presently, these international rights agencies are putting far too much emphasis on matters of piracy and copyright infringement and although these are important, international copyright should be seen as playing a positive and broadening role, rather than appear all the time to be limiting the frontiers of knowledge distribution.

We have pointed out elsewhere in this essay that many publishers in the South are not familiar with the finer points of international copyright and its collective administration. Although we are aware that some attempts have been made and are being made to increase the quantity and quality of information related to copyright and its use as well as its abuse, this information is not being made available throughout the world and at all levels. Current efforts appear to be directed mainly at governments, and we would advise that public, private, international, and other specialized publishing institutions and professional associations be included, placed on the mailing list of these agencies, and be considered for the training that is offered from time to time. The broader issues of equity and copyright control and collective bargaining and management should form part of the training awareness package offered at such courses.

The rules governing compulsory acquisition remain vague and are misunderstood by many. The majority of African publishers are ignorant of them. We are aware that there are certain provisions, brokered by UNESCO, that permit compulsory acquisition in cases where rights holders refuse to grant or unreasonably withhold copyright. Be this as it may, we are not, to this day, aware of any African publisher who has acquired rights in this way. The reasons for this include the lack of capacity referred to above, and the fact that African publishers have little knowledge on how to go about this process and which titles, if any, are available for such acquisition. Many African publishers would like to acquire rights to the writings of their first generation creative writers whose copyrights are held by publishers in the North. Often their requests are rejected outright or frustrated and delayed for reasons that can only be described as selfish and opportunistic. In some cases, these books might be prescribed as set books for schools, and thousands of copies may be required. Due to the scarcity of foreign exchange and unaffordable prices, African countries are not always in a position to buy these books abroad. It would be more meaningful for the foreign publisher to sublicense such books to a local publisher who might be able to make copies more readily available at an affordable price. It is obvious that the original publisher cannot sell such a book in as many numbers as the local publisher could. One British publisher once told the writer that he was not ready to part with his "birthright" when he received a request for a sublicense on a title by one of his African authors for sale in the East African market.

The works of Shakespeare, Dickens, Jane Austen, Tolstoy, Chekhov, Gogol, Ibsen, Brecht, Kafka, and Goethe, to name only a few, are very popular in Africa and are constantly prescribed for study in schools. African publishers have experienced problems in securing rights to these books in almost all cases. Why are the works of these long-dead literary geniuses not yet in the public domain? What should African publishers do to gain access to them? If they cannot even secure rights to the works of their own writers, what chances do they have of obtaining rights to long-established classics? This clearly is an area where a lot more work remains to be done by the purveyors of international copyright, especially KOPINOR of Norway, which is currently spending large sums of money in defense of rights holders in the United States still fighting for their "full" rights.[13]

A meaningful future strategy would call for formulation of policies at national, regional, and international levels, supported by financial and technical assistance from IFRRO, RROs, national governments, NGOs, the World Bank, and other aid agencies in the North, to strengthen African publishing industries and delink them from state control and management. Pressing issues such as lack of capital, technical and management skills, and capacity to distribute their products effectively within their own borders and for export should be tackled if an industry capable of fulfilling the educational needs of individual countries and the continent as a whole is to emerge. In other words, African publishers should be enabled to expand their capacity through full participation in the prime and relatively risk-free educational markets so that they can muster the resources to begin to devote attention to other publishing areas such as fiction, children's books, academic books, biographies, and other general and trade books that are easier to export to other markets or likely to be candidates for rights dealings. Gradually they will begin to appreciate the need to protect their intellectual property and their membership in these international copyright organizations will begin to make sense. Although such compensation would still not be adequate, at least it would go some way in correcting the present unbalanced state of affairs.

Future research projects should be initiated on a joint basis, teaming up with local and international scholars and should be guided by limited copyright protocols.[14] The findings should then be published locally or jointly with international publishers, and the copyright in those works should rest with local publishers who should originate the head contracts. There is another example in the kind of arrangement presently in force between the enterprising British publisher James Currey and several African publishers. Each party takes the market territory they think they can effectively cover, and the rest is left open for whoever gets there first. In this way, the African publisher is able not only to gain exposure outside his home market, but also garners experience in the complicated world of international copyright trading.

Thirdly, since African countries are still largely oral societies, we would urge that oral literatures and traditions be exempted from international copyright and national copyright laws in Africa. No scholar or researcher should be allowed to claim copyright on materials collected freely from rural folk, or even when certain token payments have been made for this information, or such copyrights should be limited by both national laws and international copyright conventions as suggested above. In this way, we shall be forestalling the prospect of having to seek to reclaim these copyrights from foreign researchers and their publishers in the North at a future date. And while on the issue of reclaiming copyright, we would propose that an attempt be made by African governments, publishers, and their authors to reclaim copyright in works, especially fiction, originally published outside the continent but that are now urgently required for educational purposes. Attempts to obtain sublicenses by individual publishers for certain markets have to date been less than successful.

Fourthly, African copyright laws should make it mandatory for a foreign publisher who acquires rights from an African publisher to make a full acknowledgment of this fact in his own edition. The practice will not only expose and promote the African publisher to the international market but will also affirm that he is the holder of the copyright contained in the work.

Fifthly, African governments should monitor and, if necessary, license specialized foreign book agents who come to Africa to buy rare books, including out-of-print titles and gray literature, as some of these publications may not be copyrighted, and there could be a danger that the copyrights in these books could be exported purely by the very act of buying all the copies available in Africa.

Sixthly, aware of the imbalance in the flow of copyright reproduction fees, but anxious that publishers in the South should operate within the international copyright system, some IFRRO member organizations have agreed that copyright fees collected through national RROs should, at least for the first few years, remain in that country to support publishing activities there. This is a welcome compensating message of goodwill and noble intention and should be adopted by all the national RROs currently in operation worldwide, and their 37 associate members. It is only by seeing the fruits of copyright protection that African publishers can develop confidence in the collective administration of international copyright and appreciate that it potentially stands to benefit them and that the motives of international rights holders are honorable and responsive to their welfare.

Finally, a word about the English language. English has spread to become a truly international language. Not only have the traditional English-speaking countries like the United States, Britain, and India, grown in importance among the world's major book producers, non-English-speaking countries such as Germany, the Netherlands, Sweden, Norway, and, to a smaller extent, Japan have increased their publishing output in that language. Most of the new research being carried out worldwide is done and disseminated, to a very large extent, in English. In Africa, most states have chosen English (or French) as their official language, in preference to their own languages, and have adopted it as the language of instruction in most cases after the first two or three years of primary education. The other foreign languages prevalent in Africa, namely French, Portuguese, and Afrikaans have also suffered in comparison to English—South Africa and Namibia being the latest countries to adopt it as their official language and Mozambique reportedly considering adopting it. These new realities make it necessary for international copyright conventions to adopt a softer stance to requests for same-language reprint rights in the same way as previous conventions simplified access to translation rights. Our view here is that with the growing dominance of English as a world language, same-language English reprint rights are becoming increasingly more important than translation rights.

These are only a few of the remedial measures that could be taken to stem the flight of African copyrights while functioning within the provisions of international copyright. A more permanent solution would be to subject the provisions themselves to scrutiny and to amend those sections that are inimical to the needs of the developing world. These would include considering a reduction in the duration of copyright, strengthening the clauses dealing with education exemption, compulsory acquisition, and fair dealing, simplifying the assignment of copyright clauses, and providing more effective guidelines in the treatment of oral literatures and traditions, to mention only a few.

CONCLUSION

In this essay, we have not sought to explain or interpret the various laws and protocols governing international copyright, although we are familiar with them. Rather, we have attempted, in simple and accessible language, to highlight the inherent dangers and weaknesses contained in those conventions, both in their letter and practice. We have observed that African states are faced with a choice of two evils—to sign or not to sign. They have little or nothing to benefit from signing, and little or nothing to lose by not signing. We have found no evidence of advantages or disadvantages either way, although it can be argued that by signing, book-poor African countries have compromised their human right of access to knowledge, and they will realize their folly when they will have acquired the much-needed capacity to exploit these works, only to discover that the protectionism inherent in these conventions, and sealed by their own signatures, prohibit them from doing so.

We would not advocate that African states, or the developing world, for that matter, should close their borders to the outside world, as was done by some of now developed countries, until they have achieved a level of development that would enable them to participate meaningfully in the present international copyright order, attractive though such a proposal might sound. Instead we have advocated equity, honesty, reciprocity, understanding, and fair play so that the African signatories can be compensated for the bold, courageous, and selfless step they have taken in recognition of the noble aims of international copyright conventions.

The North must realize that its continued prosperity depends to a certain extent on the developing world, Africa included, and may even be at the expense of the latter. The extent to which such a dependency relationship can be sustained is limited, now that increasing poverty in the South is already making it impossible for meaningful trade between the two blocs to take place. It is with this in mind that we have proposed that the North should accept a measure of responsibility for correcting the present imbalances, and should initiate and/or support programs (some of which have been suggested here) to strengthen the economies of African states and their publishing industries—in particular, by playing a leading role in humanizing international copyright so that it may serve the needs of knowledge dissemination more effectively and for the benefit of all.

Bibliography

African Rights Indaba 1994—Conference Papers. Harare: Zimbabwe International Book Fair 1995.

Altbach, Philip G. *The Knowledge Context: Comparative Perspectives on the Distribution of Knowledge.* Albany: State University of New York Press, 1987.

Altbach, Philip G., ed. *Publishing and Development in the Third World.* Oxford: Hans Zell Publishers, 1992.

Altbach, Philip G., ed. *Readings on Publishing in Africa and the Third Worl.* Buffalo, N.Y.: Bellagio Publishing Network, 1993.

Altbach, Philip G., Amadio A. Arboleda, and S. Gopinathan, eds. *Publishing in the Third World: Knowledge and Development.* Portsmouth, N.H.: Heinemann, 1985.

Clark, Charles *Publishing Agreements: A Book of Precedents*, 4th ed. London: Allen and Unwin, 1993.

Fennessy, Eamon T. "US Copyright Expert Goes to Nigeria and Is Impressed." *Logos* 4, no. 3 (1993): 159–61.

Flint, Michael F. *A User's Guide to Copyright*, 3rd ed. London: Butterworths, 1990.

Gopinathan, S., ed. *Academic Publishing in ASEAN: Problems and Prospects.* Singapore: Festival of Books, 1986.

Graham, Gordon. *As I was Saying.* Oxford: Hans Zell, 1993.

Gunderson, Hakon and John-Willy Rudolph. *Together As One, Seminar on Copyright and Collective Administration of Rights Within the SADCC.* Oslo, Norway: KOPINOR, 1992.

Minowa, Shigeo. *Book Publishing in a Societal Context: Japan and the West.* Tokyo: Japan Scientific Societies Press, 1990.

The Kenya Copyright Act, Cap. 130, Laws of Kenya, rev. ed. Nairobi: Government Printer, 1991. [This law is currently being amended.]

UNESCO, *Statistical Year Book* 1993. Paris: UNESCO, 1993.

6

Reading in Africa—Some Obstacles

It is difficult, even dangerous, to make general statements about Africa, a continent consisting of more than fifty sovereign states, each with its own peculiar brand of government. However, all the countries share a common colonial experience, and are involved in tackling the problems of underdevelopment, at different levels and with varying degrees of success. In this essay, I shall deal with the experiences of the liberated countries mostly in Africa South of the Sahara, and will highlight some of the obstacles facing them in the area of reading.

Reading itself has a relatively short history in Africa. It is, like most other things, a product of colonialism and the missionary activity that followed in its wake. The missionaries, more than any other agency, did much to encourage and widen the spread of reading—so much so that in most African languages the word for "reader" is synonymous with that for "Christian." The established mission presses at various centers, undertook the difficult task of transcribing African languages, taught people how to read and write, and produced for them a wide range of simple reading materials, mostly of a religious nature. Needless to say, they also taught them their own languages and made them read materials that they considered suitable for them in those languages.

As time went on, the missionaries expanded their activities—sometimes in conjunction with the colonial governments—and some ventured further into school textbook publishing. After the Second World War, commercial publishers from the metropolitan powers were encouraged to take over and build upon the foundations that had already been laid. The spread of nationalism and the resultant struggles for independence increased Africans' awareness of the value of education, which up to that time was still elitist in structure and available

---

From the *IFLA Journal* (1984).

only to the few. But the expansion of educational facilities did not come until after independence.

The new African governments inherited this hunger for education and responded by setting up more new schools for the young and launching adult literacy programs for the old. As the programs gained momentum, universal primary education was declared in some countries and in others this was even made compulsory. The level of school dropouts was checked. In order to cope with the book demands of the new school populations, state publishing houses were formed and private enterprise publishers sprang up and joined the already established multinational publishers in helping provide the books and other reading materials that were required. It did not take long for African governments to realize that they were spending nearly one-third of their national budgets on education.

International involvement in the book and reading situation in Africa has manifested itself in various ways since UNESCO convened the first meeting of African book experts, in Accra in 1968. Many other UNESCO-sponsored meetings and workshops have since been held in various African capitals with a view to formulating and developing book development strategies that can help Africa assume its rightful position in the world of book production and reading. More recently, the International Reading Association has assisted various African countries in book promotion activities intended to encourage reading and improve its quality and quantity.

Efforts within Africa itself and support from international agencies these last twenty years have produced some encouraging results. According to statistics[1] available from UNESCO, Africa's book output doubled from 4,300 titles in 1965 to 8,700 titles in 1978, and her share of world book production rose from 0.6 percent in 1955 to 1.4 percent in 1978. However, compared to the rest of the world, this output is far from satisfactory. For example, in 1978 Africa's production represented 26 titles per million inhabitants compared to 449 titles per million inhabitants in the developed world.[2]

Although this essay is about reading, I give no apologies for having gone to some length about the book situation in Africa, because books constitute a large percentage of the reading material available in any country. I have identified, for our topic today, three main obstacles to the speedy development of reading in Africa, namely *language, illiteracy,* and an *underdeveloped readership*. I shall deal with these one by one and will conclude by taking a look at the underdeveloped state of the African book publishing industry, which can be seen as both a cause and a result of the problem.

LANGUAGE

You will agree with me that if a book is to be read widely it must be written in a language spoken by a majority of the people. Unfortunately this is not the case in Africa. In most countries books are published in languages spoken by less than 30 percent of the population.

Take, for example, the case of foreign languages, in which most of the books are written. English and French, the two most widely used languages, cannot be read by more than 25 percent of the population in the countries where they are used. These foreign languages form the medium of instruction in most African countries, and books published in them stand a better chance of commercial success. But it should not be forgotten that these languages are spoken by the educated elite and that vast populations of Africa's potential reading public are cut out when we continue to publish in them. But what are the alternatives?

In a recent article, Amu Djoleto of Ghana estimates that Africa has well over 1,200 languages in use.[3] Another observer also points out that only about 600 African languages have been published in.[4] This then means that half of Africa's languages do not exist in writing, and probably have not been transcribed. Perhaps these languages are spoken by only a few thousand people and would not, therefore, be viable in written form. A lot of research would be needed into these languages, orthographies established, and grammar books and dictionaries made available before they could be useful for purposes of publishing. But then, how would this exercise serve the national interest? A country like Nigeria, for example, reported to have 350 languages would have to produce this number of translations to be able to get the same information to the whole of its population in their own languages.[5] This would create a complex situation necessitating the establishment of translation bureaus to render works from one African language into another. The ramifications would be far-reaching and too expensive to contemplate.

But this is not to say that publishing in African languages is hopeless. There are other languages spoken by millions of people and that already have a body of literature to their credit. Examples here include Hausa, Yoruba, Igbo (Nigeria), Akan (Ghana), Wolof (Senegal), Luganda (Uganda), Amharic (Ethiopia), Kikuyu and Lou (Kenya), Shona and Ndebele (Zimbabwe), Nyanja (Zambia), and Chichewa (Malawi). Unfortunately, these widely spoken African languages are also the languages of the politically dominant groups, and African governments realize the political risks of imposing them on other communities. Secondly, their written forms have not yet been sufficiently developed. Not enough research has been done to reconstruct their orthographies into authentic African sounds and symbols. When rendered in writing using orthographies inherited from the early missionaries, many of them are difficult to read and appear strange even to first-language readers. Moreover, the same observation made earlier about foreign languages is also valid in the case of these major African languages; they are not spoken by the majority of the people in any one African country.

One can perhaps find exceptions in the cases of Kiswahili in Eastern Africa and Arabic in Northern Africa. In the case of Kiswahili, spoken by approximately 60 percent of the peoples of Eastern Africa, more support is needed at every level of its usage—social, educational, cultural, economic—if it is to become the official and national language of the territory.

African countries are, therefore, faced with a language dilemma. The present practice of several languages being used alongside the languages of the former imperial powers may be expedient in the short run but it is short-sighted and costly in the long run. It is important that African governments give serious thought to the language question. An unequivocal language policy in which one language is singled out for use in the whole country would be unpopular at first, but it would eliminate wastage and make it possible for the country's resources to be geared toward developing the chosen language for the benefit of all.

ILLITERACY

The second major obstacle I wish to deal with is illiteracy. In a speech on September 8, 1982, marking the occasion of International Literacy

Day, the director-general of UNESCO reported that there were 156 million illiterates in Africa, representing 60.3 percent of the adult population. Although the level of illiteracy is still quite high, it must be acknowledged that African governments have done much in the last twenty years to fight it. At the formal education level, they have introduced universal primary education, increased the percentage of children of school-going age who actually go to school to over 65 percent, and considerably reduced cases of dropouts. At the informal level, functional literacy programs have yielded results. The Kenyan Department of Adult Education Literacy, which won the 1983 International Reading Association Literacy Award reported that more than one million people had benefited from their literacy programs. Similar programs have been undertaken in other parts of Africa, among them Tanzania, Nigeria, Ghana, and Sierra Leone, with good results.

However, many problems still remain. Shortage of money and manpower has forced several countries to extend the deadlines they had given themselves for eradicating illiteracy. During the last ten years, the heavy oil bills, the food shortages, and the challenges of coping with a fast increasing population comprised mainly of young people have forced several African countries to slow down or shelve some of their programs, adult literacy included. And with this, a new problem, namely the danger of those already rescued lapsing back into illiteracy, has become very real. The need to provide more reading materials geared to the needs and interests of the new literates has been felt though not satisfied. And for it to be satisfied adequately the problems of language discussed above would have to be solved.

Although cultural attitudes have been blamed for the slow progress of literacy in Africa, the real reasons are to be found in the economic hardships facing the continent. The recruiting and training of adult literacy teachers, the enrollment of adult students, and the provision of facilities and materials are tasks that would stretch the fragile economies of African countries.

READING

It has been widely reported that Africans do not continue with reading once formal education is completed and that they derive more pleasure from the oral and performing arts—talking, singing, dancing, and socializing—than from the rather private and individual preoccupation of reading a book. In Okot p'Bitek's celebrated work *Song of Lawino*,[6] written in Acholi in 1955, Lawino blames her husband Ocol for having abandoned the ways of his people. She accuses him of burying himself in a "dark forest of books," and allowing his manhood to be crushed "with large books."

A deeper look into the history of the book in Africa may explain how such negative attitudes developed. Firstly, when the book was first introduced, it was not promoted as something to derive pleasure from; in fact, people were forced to read it. Secondly, what they were made to read did not enrich the lives that they lived. In fact, quite often it contradicted their own beliefs and those of their forefathers, and guided them away from the majority of their own people and their rich cultural and religious heritage. Reading and education, in general, were seen as an inconvenience that had to be endured, and dispensed with when the benefits they promised had been achieved. This attitude persisted throughout the colonial period and into independence. It is my view that it will disappear gradually as basic education becomes available to all and is pursued without expectation of benefits or privileges.

So, whereas it may be true that Africans do not read for pleasure, the situation is changing fast. Readership surveys conducted during the last five years in countries like Nigeria, Benin, Ghana, Kenya, and Uganda have shown that more and more people, especially the young, are reading for pleasure. The success of some of the general books published in Nigeria, Kenya, and Zimbabwe recently has shown that Africans do continue reading after their formal education, and this reading is not purely for utilitarian purposes or achievement as is sometimes claimed.

I will, therefore, not dwell much on the so-called lack of the reading habit as being the main reason for the low level of reading in Africa. Instead, I shall highlight other factors that, in my view, militate against the emergence of a strong reading culture in Africa.

AVAILABILITY

Africa suffers from a scarcity of reading materials, whether published within the continent itself or imported from abroad. As already mentioned, the number of titles published in Africa is small indeed, and the number of those imported has been falling due to shortage of foreign exchange. In some areas, such as children's literature and adult literacy, few local books are available, and the few foreign books available are unsuitable. And finally, the price of books has increased drastically over the last ten years and is generally outside the reach of the average reader.

RELEVANCE

A lot of the books in use in Africa were not specifically designed for the African audience. Not enough research has been done to ascertain the reading interests of most Africans. Although readership surveys have already been conducted in some African countries, it is important that such surveys be conducted in all countries and more regularly so that African authors and publishers may be guided to produce books better suited to the needs of their readership. The readership survey[7] conducted among school children in Kenya in 1979 with the assistance of funds from the International Reading Association produced some interesting results. Ninety-one percent of those interviewed confirmed that they read for pleasure. Many of them preferred reading comics to storybooks. And when asked if they preferred reading stories about faraway places, or about their local area, 61 percent answered that they preferred to read about faraway places, much to the surprise of this writer.

READING EDUCATION

If more people were taught how to read well and effectively, they would probably take up reading on a regular basis. In Africa, reading education is not given sufficient emphasis. More reading teachers should be trained so that they can be utilized in improving the quality of their students' reading, both at the formal and informal levels of education. Only last May, the International Reading Association assisted in organizing a workshop in reading education at Port Harcourt, Rivers State, Nigeria—probably the first workshop of its kind on the continent. African governments are encouraged to seek assistance from the International Reading Association on how best to organize such workshops in their own countries. It is further suggested that national reading competitions be held regularly as a means of improving reading skills and inculcating the reading habit in the young. Parents who are not already doing so are encouraged to read to their children the evenings and to supervise their school reading assignments. The aim here should be to assist those who can read to develop their proficiency to the highest-possible level.

READING ENVIRONMENT

The reading habit can only develop in a situation that is conducive to reading. Most African countries do not have sufficient school or public libraries. The situation has improved somewhat from twenty years ago when some countries were reported to have no libraries of any sort. A seminar held in Abidjan, Ivory Coast, in November 1982 cited housing conditions in Africa as being unsuitable for home reading. This is true; overcrowding in certain sections of African cities, and the unavailability of power in African rural homes, add to this hostile environment.

ACQUISITION

Until recently, it was impossible for a person in one part of Africa to order a book, or obtain information about a book published in another part of Africa. These problems have now been minimized somewhat with the appearance over the last ten years of reference books such as *African Books in Print, The International African Bibliography,* and *African Book Publishing Record,* although transportation still remains a problem within the continent. However, these services are currently being provided by institutions based outside the continent itself. African countries that have not already done so are advised to set up national and regional bibliographic centers to ensure that information on books published within the country or region is readily available.

READERSHIP CAMPAIGNS

In his book *Roads to Reading*, Ralph Staiger of the International Reading Association has shown how readership campaigns have proved their effectiveness in the various parts of the world where they have been conducted, including Ghana in the African continent.[8] I understand from the association that the National Library of Nigeria, with little more than their advice and encouragement, recently organized a comprehensive readership campaign in that country. African countries could increase their reading populations if such campaigns were organized on a regular basis. Their impact is more widely felt if they are organized on a national scale and backed up with press media coverage, and with exhibitions and book-related activities going on in key places throughout the country. A follow-up publication to the one mentioned above, *Planning and Organising Reading Campaigns: A Guide for Developing Countries*, written by Staiger and Casey, and released by UNESCO in 1983, lays down detailed guidelines for those countries wishing to undertake such an exercise.[9]

THE NEW MEDIA

There has been a certain amount of apprehension in the developed world that the book and reading were under threat from the new media, such as television and video. Judging from reports of readership surveys carried out in Africa to date, this threat exists on a very small scale in the urban centers only. African countries would be well advised not to fight the new media but to harness and exploit its power in the promotion of reading, as some developed countries have done.

Problems of an Underdeveloped Book Industry

I have mentioned elsewhere in this essay that the underdeveloped state of the African publishing industry is both a cause and a result of the low level of readership on the continent. I shall now take a brief look at the writing, publishing, printing, and distribution of reading material in Africa and will make suggestions on how these can be strengthened to meet the challenges of a largely untapped readership.

Writing

Africa is not short of writers. During the last twenty years it has accumulated a battery of creative and textbook writers, and many more are struggling to be published. However, a large proportion of the books in use are written by foreigners. More support and encouragement should be given to Africans so that they can write books better suited to Africa's needs. At a UNESCO conference on "National Book Strategies for Africa," held in Dakar in 1981, several suggestions were made as to what incentives can be given. Setting up awards at the national and international level was recommended and the Noma Award for Publishing in Africa singled out for praise. The need to organize writers' workshops and to provide regular practical training for authors was underlined. Since then, writers' workshops have been held in Freetown, Sierra Leone (January 1983) and Harare, Zimbabwe (August 1983). More such workshops should be held in every country to spot new talent and direct the energies of African writers to where the real gaps are.

Publishing

Although Africa may have the potential for writing, it does not yet have sufficient publishing capability to cope with all the works written on the continent. Many African writers still publish abroad or with the local branches of multinational publishers who currently produce more titles for Africa than all the indigenous and state publishing houses put together. This is not to say that African publishers are not playing their part. Having come on the scene late, it will take them some time before they can effectively compete with their foreign counterparts. At the moment, they seem to suffer from a shortage of skilled manpower and resources. Training programs, such as the one recently undertaken by the Zimbabwe Publishing House, should be made available to all the publishing cadres—editors, translators, illustrators, designers, etc.— to enable publishing to cope with the demands of an increasing reading population. More diversified publishing houses should be set up by individual entrepreneurs and by the state, and properly capitalized to absorb the risks and capital-intensive demands of publishing.

PRINTING

The printing industry in Africa is not yet developed to a level where it can satisfy the continent's book and reading needs. Many African publishers still order their printing abroad. Not only is printing capacity inadequate, a lot of the machinery, most of which is out-of-date, suffers from constant breakdowns, and the foreign exchange to obtain spare parts is not always available. Printing inputs such as paper, inks, films, plates, threads, and stitches have to be imported as well. As a result, printing costs are too high, partly due, of course, to the very small print runs. Shortage of paper is another perennial problem. According to a UNESCO survey[10] carried out in 1979–80, Africa produced only 28 percent of the paper it consumed. This is not surprising as only ten African countries have their own paper mills and produce only certain types of paper and boards and at higher prices than those on the world market.

DISTRIBUTION

Lack of sufficient distribution outlets is one obstacle in the way of getting books to the reading population. Bookshops are few and far between and are markedly absent in the rural areas where more than 70 percent of the African population lives. As a result of this, some African governments have taken over the distribution of schoolbooks, usually the bread and butter of the bookshop business, thus further stifling the growth of a viable book trade, and creating a vicious circle in which the general reader is the victim. Transportation, especially to the rural areas, is difficult, expensive, and unreliable, putting heavy markups on the already expensive books by the time they reach the rural reader.

It must not be forgotten that the African book industry, discussed above, produces less than 50 percent of Africa's book needs, and the rest have to be imported. But the scarcity of foreign exchange, much more deeply felt these last five years, has resulted in fewer book imports, without a corresponding increase in the local output, thus further depressing reading opportunities.

However, it must be remembered that during the last thirty years, Africa has moved from a position of utter dependency on other continents for its book needs to the present position. While Africa should be proud of this achievement, it must also be recognized that the continent will depend on imported books for some time to come. In the meantime, perhaps African governments could consider waiving internal taxes and duties that some of them levy on reading materials, in contravention of the Florence Agreement to which many of them are signatories.

CONCLUSION

In this essay, I have highlighted some of the obstacles to reading in Africa—in some cases without giving suggestions for their removal. To attempt to do this would amount to a task too big to accomplish in the available space. It is worth pointing out, however, that the problems are so intertwined that they would need to be approached within the broad framework of national development policies. For example, a successful fight against poverty, hunger, disease, unemployment, and all the other ills that plague our societies, though not dealt with in this essay, would automatically change Africa's book reading and book buying habits. A campaign that brought more people into reading would, as a spinoff benefit, revitalize the African writing, publishing, printing, and bookselling industries. It is necessary, therefore, that targets and priorities for each country be worked out carefully if maximum results are to be achieved for the overall industry.

UNESCO has repeatedly urged African governments to set up

national book development councils comprising experts from all sections of the book trade. These councils, which already exist in Ghana and Nigeria, would cooperate closely and more effectively with their governments in formulating and implementing policies and programs that would help bring Africa closer to being a true reading society.

Bibliography

Altbach, P. G., et al., eds. *Publishing in the Third World: Knowledge and Development.* Portsmouth, N.H.: Heinemann, 1985.

Chavaka, Henry. *Books and Reading in Kenya.* Studies on Books and Reading, no. 13. Paris: UNESCO, 1982.

Kotei, S. I. A. *The Book Today in Africa.* Paris: UNESCO, 1981.

Staiger, R. C. *Roads to Reading.* Paris: UNESCO, 1979.

Staiger, R. C. and Claudia Casey, *Planning and Organzing Reading Campaigns: A Guide for Developing Countries.* UNESCO 1983.

UNESCO. *Towards a Reading Society: Targets for the 80's—A Program for Action.* Paris: UNESCO, 1983.

UNESCO. *Report of Regional Meeting of Experts on National Book Strategies in Africa, Dakar, Senegal, 1981.* Paris: UNESCO, 1982.

7

Book Marketing and Distribution: The Achilles' Heel of African Publishing

When I was a young publisher under British tutelage, I used to be told two things. The first was that a good book sells itself. The second was that publishing is a gentleman's profession and publishers should not debase themselves by engaging in advertising books, worse so on TV and in mass circulation tabloids. Twenty five years on, I find myself sitting in between two stools. Yes, books are different, but who cares?

The popular belief that "books are different" is under siege in this new era of liberalization, privatization, and commercialization, which has brought cut-throat competition. If I had a large marketing and promotion budget, I would advertise my books on TV and in leading commercial channels, print and electronic. New realities are propelling me in a direction I do not and did not like, having built up my career as an academic-turned-businessman, much to the consternation of my colleagues in the Senior Common Room of the University of Nairobi of the early 1970s. As I have mellowed with age, I have come to the conclusion that books are consumer products just like any other commodity, although they contain an intrinsic value that makes it necessary for the book salesman to be fully familiar with what is contained in "between the two covers," before he can confidently promote and sell them. At a recent seminar in Addis Ababa, Ethiopia, an old friend of mine from India and a seasoned publisher protested that books are not "products." Then, what are they, I ask? Should they not be promoted alongside spaghetti, soaps, medicines, or should they be discreetly advertised in colorful language to attract the unsuspecting, and sometimes ignorant buyer, like condoms?

Recently, I have been toying with the idea of advertising my books

---

This paper was written in February 1996.

on television, just like candies, biscuits, beer, cigarettes, and junk and health foods. The question I want to address here is, if I had the budget, would it be prudent for me to indulge in such high-profile gesturing? Would I sell more books as a result? Would I still retain the label of a "respectable publisher," not always driven by the vagaries of commerce? These are questions that have nagged at my conscience for a long, long time and that I shall tackle as candidly as I can in this essay, which will make a detailed survey of all aspects of book marketing and distribution in Africa, what has been tried or not tried, what has worked or not worked, and what still remains to be done.

When I joined publishing in early 1972 as a trainee editor, I was, as mentioned above, informed by my trainers that under no circumstances should I advertise books in mass newspapers and popular magazines. The best way to expose my books was to have them reviewed on radio and in newspapers. I had some difficulty identifying a regular columnist to review my books in the local newspapers. So I embarked on reviewing them myself, especially the African Writers Series fiction published in London, under a pen name. My reviews were syndicated to a sister newspaper in Dar es Salaam where they were also published. Imagine my embarrassment when I visited Dar es Salaam in 1973 and found one of my reviews in the *East African Standard* newspaper under my own byline! At that point, I decided to stop this practice. In any case, I was always being unnecessarily hard on some of my books, like Alex la Guma's *In the Fog of the Season's End*, which I gave a less than glowing review for fear of being regarded as partial. At that time, I was actively helping James Currey to assess and recommend manuscripts for publication in Heinemann's African Writers Series.

Since then, I have experimented with almost every other marketing, advertising, and promotion gimmick in the book. In some cases, I have failed miserably. In others, I have been a trailblazer ahead of my time, and some of my ideas, such as the launching of the popular fiction imprint Spear Books, have proved more successful in the hands of Macmillan, with their Pacesetters, and others who jumped on my bandwagon. I have come to the conclusion that marketing and promotion receive very low priority in African publishing programs. Most publishers consider their work complete when, after months of sweating, their book finally comes off the press.

The majority of booksellers in Africa are generally inept and do not adopt a creative approach to their business. They sit behind their counters waiting for orders to flow in. They do not engage in any promotional activity at all, and few, if any, employ salesmen. Few believe in window displays to capture the passing trade, concentrating mainly on servicing school orders. With African governments moving away from book publishing and distribution, African booksellers will find it difficult to survive, let alone thrive as they should, in a market economy. Below, I shall comment on all book promotion and marketing issues and strategies available to the African book publishing industry, making brief observations regarding the extent to which these marketing possibilities are being exploited by the African publisher today.

MARKETING AND BOOK PROMOTION OUTLETS
Market Research

Most of the books published in Africa are not backed up with thorough market research to establish the needs and interests of the would-be consumer. The majority of writers write because "this is the area of my specialization," and few bother to check if any relevant literature already exists in the marketplace. Others do so because they want to compete with a rival author or publisher whom they are convinced is "minting" money in that subject area. For example, in 1972, I decided to launch a series of students' guides to compete with the Minerva guides from India, which were very badly written, complete with potted examination questions and answers. Their (Minerva's) attempts to produce guides on African works of fiction were particularly disastrous. So I launched the series Heinemann Student's Guides, in which I have published more than 40 titles on the various prescribed set books, the majority being by African writers. Today, in Kenya, there is not a single publishing house that is not publishing student guides under one series title or another.

Then, in 1974, I launched the Spear Books series in response to worries from some of our readers and writers that the African Writers Series was far too didactic, and seemed to have been crafted specifically to capture the schoolbook market, as prescribed texts either for the "O" or "A" level examinations. This series, which I might add, did not at first get the support of my principals in London, was aimed at the lowbrow reader in search of something to read during leisure time, as opposed to going to a movie, football match, watching TV, or chatting away with a neighbor. The language was controlled and the extent was fixed between 80 to 96 pages, under the mistaken view that the African reader was young and had a short concentration span. The first five titles were published in 1975, to much critical acclaim. A deal was struck with *Joe Magazine*, at that time the most popular magazine, edited by Hilary Ngweno and provocatively illustrated by Terry Hirst. We even jointly started what appears to have been a prototype of a book club. Readers would state their preferred title(s) by completing a tear-off form and returning it to *Joe Magazine*, which would then forward the order to us for fulfillment. In spite of rave reviews, I was able to sell only 2,000 copies in the first year as opposed to my original print run of 8,000 copies, which I had hoped would be "lapped up" within the first few weeks of publication. The series continues to this day with print runs scaled down to 4,000, which normally sell out within the first two years. Today, the Spear Books series continues to grow with more than 40 titles in print, the most popular one, *My Life in Crime* by John Kiriamiti, having sold in excess of 100,000 copies.

In 1988, I invited Professor Chinua Achebe of Nigeria to assist me in launching a series of children's books, of which there were no suitable ones in Kenya. Achebe himself, in an address to the opening ceremony of the 1987 Zimbabwe International Book Fair, had described foreign-imported children's books in Africa as "poisons wrapped in between beautiful covers." I launched the East African Educational Publishers (EAEP) Junior Readers Series, with 10 books at once, four of them being Achebe's own—*How the Leopard Got His Claws*, *The Drum*, *The Flute and Chike*, and *The River*. Today, the series contains over 50 readers and is the fastest growth area in my publishing house. Achebe's launching visit was successfully followed by that of Cyprian Ekwensi, whose books *The Drummer Boy*, *The Motherless Baby*, *The Boa Suitor*, *The Passport of Mallam Ilia*, *An African Night's Entertainment*, *Juju Rock Adventure*, *The Rainmaker & Other Stories*, and *The Great Elephant Bird* have proved to be most successful with the Kenyan readers, and several of them have reprinted a few times. A couple of years ago, I invited the electrifying South African singer, storyteller, and writer, Gcina Mphlope, whose contributions to the series, *The Snake with Seven Heads*, *The Queen of the Tortoises*, and *The Singing Dog* have already won her a large following of Kenyan fans. Seeing our success in this publishing area, local firms have followed with new series of their own, the Pyramid Readers, the Anchor Readers, etc.

When the Government of Kenya decided to monopolize the publishing of primary and secondary school textbooks, have them written at the Kenya Institute of Education, and published by the state publishers, Kenya Literature Bureau, and Jomo Kenyatta Foundation, I decided to diversify my portfolio and minimize my risks by entering the "revision book" market. I launched two series, the EAEP Revision Series for primary schools, and a similar one for secondary schools. These books were very successful at first, but during the last three years, nearly all Kenyan publishers, including even the state publishers, have launched their own revision series, Gateway by Longman, Top Mark by Kenya Literature Bureau, and Gold Medal by Macmillan, to name a few.

A couple of years ago, I decided to launch a school library scheme, through which we could sell our fast-expanding series of primary readers to schools in book boxes. The idea was immediately picked up by our competitors, and there are now several schemes in operation to fulfill the library needs of rural populations. My secondary school English teacher always used to say, "Good examples will always find imitators," quoting from one of our regular readers then, *Cranes Flying South* by N. Karazen. Whereas we are happy to be copied and emulated by our colleagues, some of whom manage to do an even better job of using their international outreach and connections, we would welcome participation from our Kenyan publishing colleagues as far as researching into new ideas and projects is concerned. At present, they seem to engage in new projects essentially to give EAEP "a run for their money."

This practice of poaching ideas and industrial espionage has resulted in overpublishing in some areas, while others remain completely neglected. For example, there are no less than *four* competing primary mathematics textbooks on the Kenyan market, five in Kiswahili, three in English, five in business education, four in science, and three in arts and crafts. At the secondary school level, there is duplication in English, mathematics, Kiswahili, agriculture, and home science. The only exceptions are physics, chemistry, and biology, where there are fewer competing textbooks, the majority imported from the United Kingdom.

While competition is healthy and to be encouraged, I would urge African publishers to be original and innovative when evolving their publishing programs. It is not enough to start publishing in an area simply because you think your rival is "minting"; he might not be, and I know many cases where false information has been conveyed to rival publishers. I am currently devoting my energies and resources to developing core university texts, supplementary tertiary courses for teachers' colleges, and readers in Kiswahili. I am also actively exploring partnership and copublishing possibilities with neighboring countries in East Africa and in South Africa, India, Ghana, Nigeria, and Canada. I challenge my imitators to follow suit.

Advance Publicity Information

As far as I am aware, there is no African publisher who produces advance publicity information on new and forthcoming titles. Few bother to print promotional leaflets, and only a handful produce annual catalogues. Most of their catalogues have incomplete and outdated information, and their blurbs could do with a little editorial intervention. Usually such information comes when the book has been on the market for several months, and essential bibliographic information such as ISBN, year of publication, price, and market restrictions, etc., may be missing. Until the advent of the African Publishers' Network (APNET), the African publisher did not have a database of addresses of libraries, bookshops, and even fellow publishers to whom he could mail his publicity materials, when available. But now it is possible to obtain all this information from APNET, which has addresses of over 1,300 African publishers, 10 publishers associations, bookshops, libraries, and a host of other book-related international institutions, nongovernmental organizations, and local and international development agencies. Postage rates continue to be inordinately high, with few African countries granting special postage rates for books and other printed matter. Delays are rampant, and loss of mail is a frequent occurrence. But African publishers do know a bit more about each other and correspond together more frequently nowadays, thanks to APNET. The APNET journal *African Publishing Review*, published once every two months, is beginning to list new publications just released, and African publishers would do well to take advantage of this free service, which, incidentally, has been offered selectively by Hans Zell's Oxford-based *African Book Publishing Record* for more than 20 years.

It is absolutely essential that African publishers should get into the habit of issuing advance publicity information even for internal planning and management within their own organizations. This happens to be the cheapest and most effective way of communicating advance information about forthcoming books. Sadly, because of the vagaries and unpredictable nature of Africa's printers, there lies a danger in issuing advance information about a book, which might then take months, even years, to come off the press!

Catalogs, Direct Mail, and other Promotional Approaches

I have already referred to the paucity of catalogs and the unprofessional manner in which the African publisher prepares them, if at all. Catalogs produced by Northern publishers are glossy, handy, easy to use, with complete bibliographic information, attractively produced to catch the eye of even the most cursory passerby at any fair. The same cannot be said of African publishers, who will go to book fairs without any catalogs or outdated ones, the majority without even business cards—so that they constantly have to write their addresses on scrappy pieces of paper for their impatient customers. In some cases, the people "manning" the stands have no information about the books on display and will occasionally remove old archaic calculators from their pockets to convert their local prices into an international currency for the foreign buyer. Needless to add, few, if any, African publishers print special catalogs for book fairs with prices in convertible currencies, let alone subject catalogs for those customers with specific interests. It would be too much to expect that an African exhibitor at a book fair would have a subject and author index in their catalogs to facilitate easy reference.

As a result of their unpreparedness, African publishers lose out on a lot of orders at book fairs. And, sadly, some orders taken are not followed up on so that, six months down the road, the customer is forced to cancel his order. In a few cases, especially where the displaying publisher is a parastatal or a state publisher, the civil servant whose turn to go on an overseas trip has come simply lays out the books on the first day and goes on a shopping spree. When he comes back toward the end of the fair, he is surprised to find his books intact, almost as they were because, naturally, they are not attractive enough to tempt anyone to steal them! Not knowing how to deal with this stock, he either abandons it there for disposal by the organizers, or offers it to any library wishing to have it, free of charge, or remainders it for a song as his boxes are full of shopping and he does not want to bear the cost of freighting the books back home.

Direct mail is, in my view, the most effective way of promoting books in Africa. If you target an individual, he tends to feel honored that you have chosen him in preference to others, and will most likely respond to your mailing. In the old days at Heinemann Kenya, we used to send inspection copies to teachers and education officers, with an inspection report form inviting comments. There was a postcript at the bottom of the page to the effect that if we did not receive the reader's comments in six weeks' time, we would request him to pay for the book. The response was approximately 75 percent positive and earned us valuable intelligence and a decent inspection copy income. Unfortunately, I had to discontinue the practice because of the tedious process of sending several reminders to the reader (the latter ones usually slightly more threatening).

THEY LIGHT A LAMP AND HIDE IT UNDER A BUSHEL

Most African publishers assume that their work has been completed when they take delivery of the printed books from their printers. Yet, every publisher all over the world knows that although publication is the end of the creation process, the greater challenge lies in getting the world to know about your newborn baby. Some of the methods used in promoting and publicizing books include the following: advertising; entry into catalogs, book lists, and other national or international bibliographies; author visits and launch parties; mailing blurbs, brochures, and posters to possible sales outlets; and arranging exhibitions in schools and at special functions, for purposes of displaying one's products. Publishers will normally employ sales representatives to visit schools, bookshops, libraries, and other possible outlets for this purpose. Others will submit their new books to newspapers and magazines for review, as well as to the electronic media. Some publishers have put their catalogs on the Internet, now popularly referred to as the "electronic bookstore," for easy access by potential buyers. Needless to add, these books will contain full bibliographical information, including year of publication, ISBN, and, in some cases, coding bars. Such a situation does not exist in Africa. African publishers lack strategic and planned promotional campaigns. Some of them do not even print extra covers of their books for promotional purposes. As already pointed out, there is little or no advance information about an impending publication. Most books contain incomplete bibliographic data, and some of it may be misleading: for example, it may give a publication date that is not current, and this may discourage the buyer—particularly American academic institutions, which are always looking out for the latest publications. Some publishers do send out inspection copies, but these are usually too few in number and therefore ineffective, and little or no attempt is made to monitor their impact.

Some of these problems cannot be blamed on the African publisher, as such. As mentioned elsewhere in this essay, African publishers have little money and operate on shoestring budgets. The number of bookshops, libraries, and other institutions where they may sell their books is small indeed, and most do not have any meaningful book budgets. Transportation is slow, tedious, and expensive yet inefficient. Telephones hardly work; few firms have fax machines, which, in any case, rely on a working telephone line; the postal services are slow; the roads impassable most of the year; and their sales promotion personnel, as is true in all the other sectors of the industry, are untrained and inadequately equipped for their job.

It is our view that the African publisher has not, in spite of these handicaps, approached his job with the energy, determination, and innovativeness that would guarantee success. Several undertake publishing on a part-time basis, maintaining other equally demanding jobs elsewhere. Some invest their profits from a successful book elsewhere (e.g., buying a house or a farm, etc.), instead of ploughing them back into the business. Many will sit on their slow-moving or dead stock for a long time (a hen takes only 21 days), instead of finding ways in which they could dispose of these books, even at a higher discount or to a remainder merchant, if one exists, to improve their cash flow. Few are willing to try out methods like selling books on consignment terms so as to get them into bookshops and within reach of their customers.

The idea of going to book fairs or celebrating book events (e.g., Book Week) is relatively new in sub-Saharan Africa. In the last twenty years or so, there have been book fairs in Nigeria (Ife Book Fair), Zimbabwe (Zimbabwe International Book Fair), Kenya (Pan-African

Childrens' Book Fair), Senegal (Dakar Book Fair) and a new one is to start in Ghana from 1996. All these have been conceived and executed on an international scale. There have been book events in several other countries such as Togo, Uganda, Tanzania, Zambia, Malawi, Namibia, etc. Although the number of African participants has been increasing at these fairs, their presentation and the layout of their stands have been less than professional. Most of them do not bring catalogs, let alone visiting cards, and some appear to be unfamiliar with the products they are promoting. Others are hardly to be found at their stands, preferring instead to go shopping or visiting with their friends, or checking out long-lost relations in the host country. Last but not least, there is usually no follow-up, with contacts made, and a letter may remain unreplied to until the next book fair.

I have already commented on the quality of African-published books elsewhere in this essay. But this section would be incomplete if this issue were not revisited. It is a well-known fact that nearly 85 percent of the books published in sub-Saharan Africa are textbooks and for reasons already given, these textbooks do not travel well beyond national borders. A cursory look at most of them will reveal glaring spelling errors and bad grammar, even in the preliminary pages and the blurb. The paper used, the design, layout, and illustrations are substandard. The printing and binding are awful, displaying bad imposition on the printer's part, so that printed lines on the opposite sides of corresponding pages do not "merge." There will be "see-through" because the lines were not properly "backed-up." Uneven inking and bad registration so evident in African-produced books turn a printed page into a smudge and interfere with easy reading.

Although all these criticisms are valid, not all of them can be attributed to the African publisher, who, nevertheless, must accept responsibility for the bad quality of African-produced books. After all, it is the publisher who is the choirmaster and conductor of this mixed orchestra of players in the publishing arena. In most cases, it is he who conceives a book, identifies the author, and guides him through the writing and production process. It is he who prints the book, or puts it on tender and appoints the printer. It is he who supervises the printing, scrutinizes advance copies, and gives the final go-ahead for bulk delivery. It is he who pays the printer, and offers the book for sale. He is at the center of the book chain, and even though he may not be the one who makes the most money in this game, publishing as we know it today would not exist without him. Some people have described the publisher as a "midwife." This definition is partly valid as far as the creation side of the chain is concerned, but when one considers the investment side of the venture and the risks involved, and the number of "children" he has to midwife everyday, one realizes that the publisher is not only a midwife, but the mother, father, nurturer, guardian, promoter, and final undertaker of the book "child."

Factors with which the African publisher must contend include impatient and inexperienced authors with overblown egos; lack of professional training for both author and publisher; untrained and inexperienced printers, working with archaic Heidelbergs, some more than a century old; and lack of proper quality controls and discipline at all levels of the African book publishing chain. How else could one justify a book that is put on the market without a date of publication, an ISBN, and crucial factual information that librarians and other book buyers all over the world are guided by in their purchasing? How could a decent book be published without a blurb or any spine lettering? Admittedly, Africa does not yet have designers who can produce covers that "beckon" the passerby and "invite" him to look at them. Admittedly, most African countries do not have access to good laminating and spirit-varnishing equipment to say nothing of bindery lines with proper tropicalized glues and cover-scoring facilities. Even then, our view here is that African publishers are not producing their best out of this admittedly bad technological situation.

With the current mood of liberalization and commercialization, African publishers should begin to explore possibilities of printing their books in countries such as Mauritius, South Africa, Zimbabwe, and Kenya (in that order), whose printing and packaging industries are capable of producing books that one could proudly exhibit at Frankfurt, Bologna, and other internationally recognized book fairs. It would be foolish to exhibit textbooks at such fairs, however well known and profitable they might be in your home market. The whole area of trade and general publishing is even more complex and calls for even better technical and production skills. For the moment, African publishers should devote their energies to publishing more attractive children's books for their home, regional, and continental markets. General books, including fiction, do well where there is a developed middle class with more time for leisure and a disposable income. African countries have yet to reach this level and would be well advised to stay within the school textbook and simple children's book publishing bracket.

DISCOUNTS AND RELATED CREDIT TERMS

This is, without a doubt, the most controversial question in book distribution and one about which no one is yet agreed, including our Northern torchbearers. I remember witnessing an acrimonious exchange between two of the largest British publishers at Queen Elizabeth II Hall, in London, the scene of the International Publishers Association conference in 1990. The speakers, Ian Chapman and Paul Hamlyn, lost their tempers on the set. The latter was nervously fidgeting but not surrendering an inch in their discussion of retail price maintenance in the United Kingdom. I believe Paul was advocating that the forces of supply and demand be allowed to establish the percentage discounts publishers should give to distributors. I have felt strongly that such an approach would seriously damage the ability of small, countryside booksellers competing with the big High Street bookshops and merchandising houses. In the absence of a truce, which the session's chairman failed to broker, it would appear that Paul won the day, with Ian's concluding remarks being "over my dead body."

There are many players in the book marketing and distribution chain, each claiming to play a significant and unique role, and all apparently depending on each other to ensure the success of a publication. These include the wholesalers (distributors), the retailers (bookshops), and the merchandising houses (such as the bookshops in large department stores—Debenhams, Sainsbury's, Tesco, Asda, and Marks & Spencer, to name only a few in the United Kingdom. These outlets also operate different discount structures, ranging from the volume of the purchase to the terms of credit (e.g., cash, 30 days, 60 days, etc.). One such large buyer can insist on a discount as high as 75 percent and might request that the publication be repackaged to suit the needs and tastes of his market niche. The next category consists of bona fide bookshop chains such as W. H. Smith, Waterstones, and Dillons, which may operate as trade or educational bookshops. The rest are the types of small bookshop chains one finds all over the world, with some of them running a few shops, or even only one shop in a particular area. These are the ones Ian Chapman was trying to defend and lost because "small is beautiful" gave way to "big is beautiful" when British publishers started engaging in mergers and paper sale transactions whose main achievement was to put a lot of ill-gotten wealth into the hands of a few British publishers, Paul Hamlyn himself being a good example. A viable and vibrant publishing company would be bought by these sharks, stripped of its assets, trimmed down so that the "unprofitable" parts of its list are scaled down or discontinued or even sold off. The result would be a "lean and mean" company, healthy in every respect, which would then be publicly quoted on the stock exchange. The value of the stocks would increase substantially and these speculators would then cash some of the premiums thus gained, and use the newly acquired profits to stalk another company. It is through such practices under Thatcherism that millionaires like Paul Hamlyn increased their wealth tenfold without even touching or going through the daunting exercise of deciding whether or not to risk investing in a new book, or to what extent one should continue publishing in unprofitable but essential subject areas such as drama and poetry. It is against this background that my employer Heinemann Educational Books Ltd., then a member of the Thomas Tilling Group of Companies, changed owners four times in less than two years and the East African branch was eventually offered to me to buy because it was "unprofitable" and Africa was a risky area to operate in.

Perhaps a word should be said about secondhand bookshops, remaindering, and merchandising houses. Some British and American publishers have policies to destroy, remainder, or sell off, at very high discounts, books (especially fiction, children's books, etc.) that do not sell off or prove their worth within the first eight weeks or so of publication. These books are then usually bought by the large department stores referred to above, which may be able, through their enormous sales and publicity budgets and their many outlets, to sell these stocks at a handsome profit. They have no problem in outpricing small booksellers, and this is the injustice that Ian Chapman was trying to expose to the international book community. I was very surprised that these two urbane publishing giants (Hamlyn as chairman of Reed Books and Chapman as chairman of Collins), had chosen to wash their white linen in the august Queen Elizabeth II Hall. But this shows just how sensitive the issue of discounts and retail price maintenance on books is, and how difficult it is to reconcile all the interests involved.

In Africa, there are no rules in this game of discounts, which generally vary between 15 and 40 percent. There are no large department stores with book sections, no merchandising agents, no remaindering houses, and very few trade, educational, institutional, or privately owned bookshops. The few that exist are based mainly in the urban areas, supplying to a small catchment area. There are hardly any bookshops in the rural areas, as these areas are far too remote and without access roads, rail, or postal services. Most booksellers are undercapitalized, ill-trained, and ill-equipped. They have neither the capacity nor capability to cater for the needs of their clientiele, which consists mostly of school teachers, pupils, and specialist groups. Only churches have what one might describe as a chain of bookstores, but these normally concentrate on selling the Bible, hymn books, and other Christian literature. The greatest problem facing African booksellers is that they are not accessible to their would-be customers; they lack some of the key titles their readers may be looking for, and are sometimes forced to mark up their prices beyond the reach of their readers in order to cover their costs, paying excessive postage and transportation charges while operating within a small and inflexible discount structure. Publishers cannot afford to improve their discounts because they are operating on very expensive borrowed money (if they can get it), print in small and nonviable runs, and do not have the budgets, capacity, or ability to promote their books. The low sales recorded by African publishers mean that the royalties they pay to their authors are not high enough to encourage them to take writing seriously. It is a vicious circle, one that is difficult to break out of without tackling the larger problems of poverty and underdevelopment.

The proceeds from the book publishing business in Africa are too small to be beneficially distributed among the principal players involved. Authors complain of small royalty percentages and earnings; and the publishers' low margins have resulted in losses, negative cash flow, and bankruptcies. In Kenya, for example, although the discounts extended to distributors and retailers have increased from around 20 percent to nearly 40 percent in the last 25 years, they still complain that their transport and other overhead costs leave them with little or no margins. As far as we are concerned, the solution does not lie in extending further discounts to distributors. More emphasis must be put on widening the market base of African countries by adopting policies that will bring about increased literacy, improved disposable income levels, and encourage book reading and book buying habits by building more libraries and reading centers, and generally doing everything possible to create, develop, and sustain a reading environment. Greater book consumption will result in greater sales for bookshops, more library activity, more books published, and a larger purse for the author.

BOOK DEVELOPMENT COUNCILS

The idea of book development councils (BDCs) was first mooted by UNESCO as a panacea for solving book development problems in developing countries—mainly in the South, but in the North as well. In the mid- to late 1960s, BDCs were established in Asia and South America largely through the initiative of influential local and upcoming publishers in those countries. Those initiatives were largely successful on both those continents. Today, more than 15 countries in Asia have fully functioning BDCs, and at least half a dozen countries in Latin America operate equivalent book institutes. The objective of BDCs is, to quote Abul Hasan, "to stimulate and co-ordinate the publication and use of books in such a manner that they become effective tools of national development and to integrate book promotion plans into overall national, development planning. The council should provide a national focal point which might serve both as a clearing house on publishing policy and as a centre where production and distribution problems could be kept under continuing study."

UNESCO's success on these two continents prompted it to replicate the same strategy for Africa following the Accra meeting of 1968. It played a key role in the establishment of a regional book council in Yaounde, Cameroon, in 1974. CREPLA, for this was the French acronym of the Centre for the Promotion of Children's Publications in Africa South of the Sahara, was launched with much fanfare, with the OAU and African governments pledging full support. But the project turned out to be a sitting duck. By 1984, CREPLA, under the leadership of Mr. William Moutchia, had little to show for its existence. Moutchia blamed this on lack of definition of the goals and mission of the center. He also claimed that the support promised by the OAU and his own country had not been forthcoming. But there seemed to be enough funds available in the early 1980s to enable Mr. Moutchia to travel to almost every book event in Africa and beyond, expounding and promoting CREPLA's mission and vision, and appealing for support from Northern governments and international development and donor agencies, as well as African governments. He was not successful with any of these appeals, and CREPLA started to die a slow death, with support coming in only from his own home country, Cameroon, where the center is domiciled.

Although there is still mention of CREPLA at international gatherings, the center is moribund, and has little to show for its many years of existence. At a recent publishing seminar in Addis Ababa, Ethiopia, we were informed that CREPLA has become an embarrassment even to the Cameroonian government itself, as it has achieved and continues to achieve nothing while continuing to be supported by the Exchequer. "Our baby has become an embarrassment," said the Cameroonian delegate, "and we now have three options, to dissolve it, privatize it or turn it into an NGO." One project that was initiated by CREPLA at the behest of UNESCO was publishing children's books for Africa, using the same artwork to produce several national editions of the same book, with local languages providing the text and/or captions. Eighteen years down the road, only three children's books had been identified for coproduction and only one *Chaka* had been published in only two languages, English and French. The copublisher chosen to publish the East African edition had neither the capital, know-how, or experience to produce and market children's books successfully, although he managed to launch it at a lavish party at the Hotel Intercontinental in Nairobi, with Mr. Moutchia in attendance.

The failure of the CREPLA experiment can, in my opinion, be attributed to three factors, namely: bad management at the Secretariat, lack of support from African governments, loss of follow-up interest by UNESCO and other donor and development agencies, and the fact that Africa did not have a Noma who could have propped it up and supported it financially when UNESCO finally developed cold feet. Even more important is the fact that the concept of BDCs was UNESCO-driven and totally ignored the existence of the local publishers that were then emerging and preferred, instead, to work with African governments. And this was the recipe for disaster, mismanagement, inertia, bureaucracy in decision making, dwindling support from the donors on the grounds that "the centre, so far, had nothing to show to justify its continued existence." It was a noble idea, with the right mission and purpose, but it was far ahead of its time. I am not convinced that, even now on the eve of the 21st century, a project such as this can succeed in Africa. African publishers just do not have the capital to invest in order to support and develop such an idea when the donor or development agency project circle comes to an end and the funds dry up.

To date, BDCs exist in Ghana, Nigeria, Zambia, Namibia, and South Africa. They are more effective in the countries where they are headed by a book person from the private sector. They are ineffective where they are headed by a nonprofessional public or civil servant. For a book chain to work, authors, artists, graphic designers, translators, publishers, printers, booksellers, book users, and libraries— be they public, parastatal, institutional, or private—must work in tandem with their governments through the ministries of education, culture, commerce, finance, and information and broadcasting. The person in charge should have the status, knowledge, skill, experience, strategy, and alertness that only a conductor of a large orchestra has. There is no such person in Africa today, and cash-strapped UNESCO, for all its good intentions, simply does not have the capacity or the will to work with African book professionals in a fast-growing private sector-driven publishing industry. As long as UNESCO continues to operate through governments in Africa, its noble efforts will come to nought. As long as it continues to hatch grandiose schemes from Paris and without consultation with those whom it is supposed to serve, it will not have the local goodwill and support necessary to enable it to achieve its mission and goals.

UNESCO should realize that its programs worked best in centrally controlled governments, especially in Eastern Europe, Southeast Asia, and South America. In today's world where commercialization, privatization, and sustainability are the benchmark, the bottom line is the most important determinant of the viability of any project. UNESCO must adapt to these changes or else its role in the field of education and culture will progressively diminish. And African governments must realize that the burden of providing services to their peoples is their responsibility and not that of donors (the World Bank in particular, nongovernmental organizations, and other international development or donor agencies). To achieve this, African countries should resort to less government, and empower their own people to take charge of their economies and general welfare. Unless and until these issues are seriously addressed at relevant international and regional forums, and a longer-term strategy for their resolution put in place, Africa has neither the goodwill, policies, superstructure, nor infrastructure that can meaningfully provide a sustainable solution to the problem of book provision in Africa.

NATIONAL PUBLISHERS ASSOCIATIONS

One country that has made effective use of its national publishers association (NPA) is Great Britain. Working closely and in tandem with the British government, its BDC, which was earlier on privatized and renamed International Book Development (IBD), this organ works hand in hand with the British Council, which is the de facto cultural and educational wing of the British Foreign Office. The aims are simple and noble—namely, to promote and facilitate the widest possible use of the English language throughout the world. These efforts have been very successful. Propped up by organs like the British Publishers Association, the Copyright Clearing Centre, the Arts Council, *The Bookseller*, and numerous trusts and other philanthropic organizations, the IBD has, over the last 50 years, almost converted English into a world language. There is nothing wrong with this. After all, it has enabled several important international conferences to be conducted without the intervention of translators, who are very expensive to hire and are sometimes unfamiliar with the topic under discussion, and slow or even unable to convey the jokes and cultural nuances of simultaneously translated speeches and interventions.

The commercial and cultural upshot of this is that the need for English-language facility has expanded tremendously over the same period. Now we hear of English-language teaching, English as a second language, English as a foreign language, and all sorts of other schemes that have benefited British publishers since they are best placed to provide the relevant books and related materials to support these programs. In less than 20 years, British publishers have been able to reap fortunes from these programs in nontraditional English-language markets such as the Middle East, Spain, Italy, Egypt, and Japan and are now spreading out to the newly democratized countries of Eastern Europe, Indonesia, Malaysia, and China, not to mention India and the Southeast Asian subcontinent. English has, without any doubt, become the acknowledged lingua franca of the world, with African countries such as Namibia, South Africa, and Cameroon now admitted into the

Commonwealth, and Mozambique and Angola expressing a wish to join. I cannot imagine for a moment that a meeting of the countries of the Commonwealth would require translation services, so the non-English-speaking countries that have expressed a wish to join the Commonwealth have willingly subjected themselves to the English language. Tanzania, which, for a long time insisted on the use of Kiswahili at all levels of its education system, has succumbed to the might of the English language and is now gradually introducing English as the official medium of instruction. The latest country to convert to English is Rwanda, where English is to replace French as the official language. But one should remember that all this brings with it cultural, commercial, social, economic, and political implications. Is it proper that English should become the language of the world? What would be the dangers of this? In the face of the support of the United States, the undisputed world superpower, efforts by France, Germany, Spain, Italy, and Portugal to sell their languages abroad have not been successful. They simply do not have the infrastructure, superstructure, and financial backing that the English language currently enjoys. It is a fait accompli that English will be the master language of the world for some years yet, and this will put more money in the pockets of British publishers, especially the multinationals. In Africa, the situation is quite different. Only 10 countries—namely, Nigeria, Ghana, Ethiopia, Kenya, Uganda, Tanzania, Zimbabwe, Zambia, Namibia, and South Africa have national publishers associations, Ethiopia's being the youngest, created only several weeks ago.

As I pointed out earlier, only Ghana, Nigeria, Zimbabwe, Tanzania, Namibia and South Africa have book councils. Both the book councils and national publishers associations are heavily influenced and controlled by government, except in the case of Nigeria, Ghana, Zimbabwe, Namibia, and South Africa. Looking at these statistics, it becomes obvious that the most successful African publishing countries are those that are free from government control and direction. The case of Kenya invites debate. Kenya was among the countries that attended the first publishing conference, held in Ghana in 1968, organized and sponsored by UNESCO. At that meeting, it pledged to start a book council immediately—as reported by the Kenyan delegate, Francis Pala, then director of the Kenya National Library Service. At a UNESCO meeting in 1972, Kenya reported that it had already set up a book council. The truth, however, is that the Kenyan Book Council was not registered until 1982, and a certificate for this registration exists. The sad thing is that the Kenyan Book Council exists in name only to this day, in spite of promises from the Ministry of Education and the Kenya National Commission to UNESCO that an act of Parliament to give statutory status to the Kenya Book Council is before Parliament. A UNESCO-organized conference was held in Nairobi in 1988, and its theme was "Re-launching the Kenya National Book Development Council." Several recommendations emerged from the meeting and the Ministry of Education promised UNESCO and the delegates that a council would be formed at once. But, to this day, nothing has happened. Even then, my fear is that such an organ, when created, will be headed by a bureaucratic civil servant with little or no knowledge or empathy with the Kenyan publishing industry.

The story of the Kenyan national publishers association is different. The Kenya Publishers' Association (KPA) was registered in January 1971. At that time, it was primarily controlled by expatriate publishers working for local branches of multinational publishers. KPA has had a checkered career, and in the year 1982, it split into two parts, with local indigenous publishers breaking away to form the Society of Kenya Publishers. Through my 10-year tenure as chairman of a divided and extremely antagonistic organization (1982–1992), I was able to bring back some of the breakaway partners. My finest hour was in 1990 when I was able to persuade Alexis Koutchoumow, secretary general of the International Publishers Association (IPA), to recommend KPA for membership in the international body. I no longer serve on the KPA Executive, but I continue to work closely with it and participate fully in its programs. As an African, I have received the rare "honor" of being invited to serve on the Executive Committee of the IPA, the International Committee, the Freedom to Publish Committee, and am a regular panelist at meetings of the Reading Committee. This, together with my involvement with the African Books Collective, African Book Publishing Record (ABPR), African Publishers' Network (APNET), Friends of the Book Foundation, Bellagio Group of Donors, Council for the Promotion of Children's Science Publications in Africa, the Pan African Children's Book Fair, the Dag Hammarskjold Foundation, and the Canadian Organization for Development through Education, has enabled me to play my part in Kenyan, African, South, North, South-South, and North-South publishing programs and strategies aimed at strengthening and empowering the publishing industry in Africa and the developing world. The Kenyan publishing industry is struggling to succeed in spite of the many hurdles being placed in its way by the Kenyan government, and its failure to cooperate fully with the other countries in the region in the establishment of a common East African market. If the socialistic, autocratic, and monopolistic policies adopted by the Kenyan government after the adoption of the Mackay Education Report in 1981 had been put in place at independence, Kenya would today be a disorganized book-poor nation, just like other African countries. In the new spirit of commercialization, liberalization, and privatization, Kenya needs less government and more enlightened information, publishing, and book policies, if it is to regain its glory as a leading publishing and knowledge center in Africa, a position it enjoyed in the late 1960s and early 1970s.

Conclusion and Recommendations

The problems of book marketing and distribution in Africa are part and parcel of the problems of African publishing itself. Some of these problems result from underdevelopment and are not within the publishers' ability to solve. Any approach to solving these problems must be holistic because the publishing chain fails when any of its components fails. In conclusion, we shall attempt to put forward proposals that, if put in place, would not only successfully tackle the problems of marketing and distribution, but would also strengthen the African book publishing chain itself. Our view is if the African publisher is to be empowered and enabled to deliver, the following five issues need to be addressed: policies, infrastructural development, access to funds, market expansion, and overall economic development.

Policies

Most African countries continue to function without any policies whatsoever in this vital and fast-growing area of communication. A few may have an education policy, information policy, book or publishing policy, press law, or a book council. In terms of policy formulation,

Namibia, South Africa, Nigeria, and Ghana appear to have made some progress. It is no wonder that these are the fastest-developing countries in Africa, as far as publishing is concerned. Their book industries operate in tandem with mainstream government policies and their national publishers associations and book councils work closely with their ministries of education and culture. Putting aside the issue of state versus private-enterprise publishing, African governments must formulate policies that can enable publishing to develop within a mainstream national development strategy—otherwise we shall create, as we have already done, unnecessary structures, some of which may conflict with, duplicate, or even contradict our stated objectives. It is my view that publishing thrives better in the private sector, due to its very personalized yet professional style as well as the complications of administering a small but complex organization with many "product lines"—each book constituting a product line on its own. It would be impossible for such an industry to be controlled centrally unless, of course, it is done in the way communist Soviet Union used to do it— by treating every book in exactly the same way, so that the number of copies printed and "sold" was always the same for every book published. In these days of liberalization and privatization, African governments should give serious consideration to controlling education by preparing and approving curricula, and by assessing and advising schools on the strengths and weaknesses of new books appearing on the market. In this way, they will be able to control the quality of education they offer without having to engage in commerce.

Infrastructural Development

Here we are thinking of services such as communication networks— roads, railways, sea routes, airlines—housing and rural electrification; schools and library development; and tertiary and higher institutions of learning. These are the services that must be in place if a publisher's work is to be made easy, and if he is to get his books to all parts of the country, especially the rural areas. This infrastructure is inadequate in most of Africa. Unfortunately, there is little the African publisher can do in such a situation, and this is what creates book marketing and distribution headaches. The growth of infrastructures mentioned above is concommitant with general national development. A more-developed country like South Africa has a thriving book industry, while the economic development taking place in Zimbabwe, Namibia, Kenya, and Ghana can be seen from their fairly active book industries. Undeveloped countries such as Mozambique and Angola have no book industries to speak of, while others such as Uganda, Tanzania, Zambia, and Malawi are still struggling.

We can also include, under the this heading, the infrastructure needed for book creation, production, and distribution. A publishing industry requires the support of good writers, publishers, designers and artists, printers, bookshops, and libraries. The absence of one, or the inadequacy of any of these players, affects the rest.

While advising that African governments should stay out of trading in books, I would urge them to give attention to developing a proper infrastructure that can support publishing and other commercial activities on a national and regional scale. Here, we shall also recommend the strengthening of national, regional, and continentwide lobby groups that support and represent the publishing industry. APNET should be strengthened, supported by national governments and granted diplomatic status in OAU-member countries. National publishers associations should be established in countries where they do not exist, and should operate in tandem with government policies but as separate independent organs. Book councils should be set up on a national and regional basis, along the lines recommended by UNESCO. However, our view is that they should not be headed by civil servants, nor be made to report to a government ministry, although relevant government ministries should be represented on such councils. Regional groupings such as PTA, COMESA, IGADD, and SACO in Eastern, Central, and Southern Africa and WAC and the Federation of French-Speaking African Countries in West and North Africa should be strengthened so that they can work toward improving regional contacts and trade within Africa. Regional examining bodies and literature bureaus similar to those set up by the colonial governments soon after the Second World War should be reestablished with a view to strengthening local publishing and supporting publications in minority languages, especially indigenous African languages.

Finance

Indigenous African publishers are undercapitalized. They get no assistance from their governments, and most banks view them with suspicion. There is no bank in Africa, to our knowledge, that will accept publishers' stock as collateral at full value. International aid and development agencies are only now beginning to take an interest in African publishing, and the World Bank and ODA are gradually beginning to accept that African publishers have sufficient capacity to bid for, win, and supply some of their tenders. Previously, their tenders of books destined for Africa used to be published in Europe and America, usually without the knowledge of commercial publishers in the recipient country. Lack of money is still the African publisher's greatest problem. He cannot afford to hire, train, and retain high-caliber staff. He has no funds for prepublication research, advance publicity material and postpublication activities such as advertising, launch parties, posters, and other publicity gimmicks. The quality of his books is inferior as he has no alternative but to go for cheap alternatives. Most of his books will be in paperback, with a simple black-and-white cover, and where he can afford full color on the cover, he does not give it the full complement of lamination or spirit varnishing. Due to cash flow problems, he engages in short-term projects that can bring in immediate gains but are not sustainable. In other words, he would prefer to publish revision books than engage in an expensive but potentially profitable textbook project. If the African publisher could find a source of cheap money, the quality of his books would dramatically improve as would his general demeanor and that of his publishing house.

Economic Development

The point has already been made that although books are everywhere in Africa regarded as essential commodities, preference is given to other day-to-day living needs such as food, health, housing, clothing, and school fees. The reason for this is visible and immediate, the damage caused by lack of knowledge and information is not visible and its effects are not immediate. There are many people living their lives today without reading the daily newspaper, let alone a book. And while people in the developed world are communicating through the information superhighway—the Internet, e-mail, fax, and other highly developed telecommunications equipment—some communities in Africa are still basically oral. There is talk in the North about a "bookless" society, meaning a postbook society, while for us in Africa, "bookless" societies are indeed prebook societies. So, unless Africa achieves a rate of economic development that will leave its people with disposable incomes, decent living and working conditions, and some leisure time, book buying habits may not develop even if the publisher were to have sufficient funds to engage in the book promotional activities mentioned above.

Market Development

African publishing has a very narrow market base. Most African books are published in foreign languages (e.g., English and French) that, in most cases, are spoken by minority groups. Africa has over 1,000 languages, and a majority of them do not yet have transcribed orthographies. Moreover, more than 50 percent of Africans are illiterate and therefore have no need for books. The problem of lack of book reading and book buying habits in Africa has been widely publicized and was referred to earlier in this essay. Most of the books on sale in African bookshops are imported from Britain and France and do not deal with the issues that interest African readers. Many find them fickle and irrelevant and an affront to their own culture. Elsewhere, we have already referred to the lack of a reading environment, and have emphasized the need for rural libraries and rural electrification. Finally, we can only reiterate that for a sustainable book market to emerge in Africa, we should not only address the questions raised above but should work hand in hand with our governments in order to bring about economic development. One attends to one's basic needs first before buying a book. So if we can improve the economies of African countries, their people will gradually accumulate the disposable income needed for buying books and other items of value.

In closing, we have revisited the wider problems and issues affecting publishing in Africa. Marketing and distribution are part of the publishing process, and it would have been foolish to tackle this subject in isolation. Although marketing and distribution come at the end of the publishing chain, they are, in our view, the determinants of the success or failure of any publishing business.

8

Pricing Publications

Pricing is part and parcel of the publishing process. It involves all departments of the publishing outfit, although in most cases it is vested in the editorial department, as the editor is in the best position to know all the costs involved in book production. However, in some organizations pricing of reprints could be done in the production department or, in the case of agency work, in the distribution department. The accounts department operates in close liaison with other departments and normally plays its part before, during, and after pricing.

But why must publications be priced? One reason is to enable books to be sold to the public at a uniform price. Another is to control book prices and ensure that the public buys them at fair prices. Some government departments insist on prices being indicated on books and go so far as laying down costing and pricing formulas for book producers and sellers. As we shall see later in this paper, pricing of publications is so complicated that I do not know of any case where a theoretical formula for pricing publications effectively and meaningfully has been successful.

LOCALLY GENERATED PUBLICATIONS

Typesetting and Film

These are what would normally be called the costs of origination or investment. These costs would remain fixed regardless of the number of copies to be printed. They obey the economies of scale and contribute to the variation in unit cost. For example, if you print a few copies,

---

Paper presented to the Second Annual Conference of the Association of African Science Editors, Gaborone, Botswana (1986).

the cost is amortized over that number and if you print five times more copies, the origination cost will be spread over that large printing quantity.

Materials

This is the largest of all the cost inputs. It includes things like paper, plates, threads, or stitches. The cost of materials in most cases will average between 55 and 65 percent of total production costs, particularly in developing countries where most of these things have to be imported.

Printing

This is the unit cost of printing and publication. Sometimes, in cases where the publisher does not hold paper stock it may be difficult to separate it from the cost of materials. Here again, economies of scale come in—the more you print, the lower the unit cost. The quality of the materials used also plays a part, particularly the quality of the paper used, the preferred binding, the finishing process, etc.

Royalty

This is an agreed fraction taken from revenue or from the publishing price that is payable to the author. This can vary from anything like 2.5 percent of published price (or receipts) to 20 percent. Royalty has a dramatic effect on the pricing of publications and should always be realistically negotiated. In cases where the publisher pays a straight fee to the author, this fee should be considered when pricing a publication.

Trade Discount

This discount is given to a distributor or retail bookseller so that he can sell your books at the recommended price. It can vary from 10 to as high as 65 percent, even 70 percent, depending on the type of book, and the type of buyer. Normally, individual buyers will pay the full price, institutions may get some discount, booksellers would get a discount in the region of 20 to 40 percent, and a publisher buying from another publisher might expect upwards of 50 percent, inclusive or exclusive of royalty.

The Life of a Publication

This point is related to materials and printing costs. If you want to launch into the market cheaply or if there is vigorous competition, you might deliberately underprice your book in order to break into the market. If you do this, you should always think about the life of the publication first. There are printers who will agree to print 10,000 copies at the price that they would normally charge for 20,000 copies, but only if you can convince them that your book will have a long life and that you will shortly be going back for a reprint. Generally, it is advisable to order quantities on the conservative side as you can always go back for a reprint. If you print too many copies at the outset, you might be exposing yourself to the danger of dead stock in future. This prerogative of negotiating special prices with the printer must be exercised with care, a thorough salability study must be carried out if you are to win the confidence of your printer—otherwise if you continue to make mistakes he will not listen to you.

The Do-It-All Yourself Publishers

There are some publishers who prefer to write, print, and sell their own publications. Personally, I would discourage this approach because no one can be an expert in everything. However, should one insist on this approach, then I would recommend that all the costs incurred should be recorded carefully so that the viability of the business is periodically put to test. The publisher should work out the cost centers so that he can know his weaknesses, and that if need be he can resort to professional help in one or two of the functions arrogated to himself. But from the cases I have seen, one factor always seems to make unfair or unrealistic demands on the other. For example, you could be forced to print a second-rate novel on your machines, just because you have idle capacity, and so on.

Pricing of Imported Books

The most important factor in pricing imported books is the discount you are able to get, and what other terms you are able to negotiate (e.g., royalty inclusive or exclusive, closed or open market arrangements, etc.). Your landed cost (i.e., unit cost plus freight) would then become the basic cost upon which you are to calculate your selling price, remembering that your distributor will expect the usual discount, or commission. It is possible to determine all the cost centers with precision, so that you are able to know exactly which costs should be included in an imported publication and which should not. This point will be dealt with when we get to the actual mechanics of pricing below.

The Mechanics of Pricing

The actual mechanics of pricing is explained in a paper I presented to a conference organized by the Dag Hammarskjold Foundation in Arusha, Tanzania, in 1984. (See Appendix at the end of this essay for a demonstration of this costing process.) In addition, it is essential to respond to the needs of the market and to the competition, which should form part of your long-term and short-term strategies. It is important to remember that every decision you make—print quantity, materials to be used, royalties, discounts, etc., all impinge on pricing.

Generally, the publisher should aim at an average net profit of 15 percent, or at least the margin should be above the local bank interest rate. The royalty payable should be negotiated between 5 and 15 percent depending on the caliber of the author and the importance of his publication. The discount to booksellers and distributors should be in the region of 20 to 35 percent, and the average gross margin should always be upwards of 50 percent and, advisedly, not over 55 percent on a first issue, as you can expect a better margin on reprints. In aiming to achieve a 15 percent net profit you should keep your costs below 35 percent of the receipts from your publications.

As the book you are selling could be a locally generated one or an imported one, I would venture to suggest that it is advisable to further identify the cost centers in your firm on a departmental basis. This would have the advantage of giving you a clearer picture of your performance in each department and would provide you with a method of checking and containing costs and would also enable you to approach every publication offered to you as flexibly and as sensibly as possible.

Let us take a hypothetical case of an organization whose net profit is 15 percent and whose costs are 35 percent. Upon close scrutiny, the cost centers can be established as follows:

Management	9%
Sales	11%
Distribution	9%
Editorial	6%
Total	35%

A company that has refined its cost distribution would be in a better position to respond more flexibly to a request for editorial, sales, or distribution services if requested to do so by somebody who has already met some of the costs of publication.

Even if you are a charitable or a non-profit-making parastal, you need to determine all these cost centers if you are to remain afloat and to develop in any orderly manner. Needless to say, good management and professionalism are the main factors for surviving in any market.

PRICING PROBLEMS

Every pricing exercise assumes a certain life of the publication, under particular given circumstances. Problems arise:

- when the publication does not sell in the time period provided. In a case like this you may be forced to increase your price, or if you end up with dead stock, you may be compelled to pulp the books. If you operate in a price-controlled market where you are required to print the price on the book, you would find yourself in the embarrassing position of having to block your own prices with a sticker! And if it should take you longer to sell the initial stock than you had budgeted for at the outset, you would find reprints very difficult to cost and might be forced to let the book go out of print.
- where currency fluctuations abound. This affects both locally generated books and, even more so, imported books. The devaluation of currencies, so rampant in Africa, would force the publisher to increase prices higher than those previously announced, as imported books take anywhere from 6 months to 12 months to arrive at their destinations, during which time such fluctuations may have occurred.
- in those countries where there are strong price control regulations and/or publishers are required to print prices on their publications. This point is related to the first two circumstances described above. Where copyright law is not respected, allowing other people to reproduce your publications without due acknowledgment or compensation, the originating publisher is likely to find himself with higher prices for his book than the publisher who has simply reproduced them.
- where piracy abounds. The pirates will price their publications lower since they do not pay origination costs and royalties.
- where unscrupulous markups are allowed. Distributors and booksellers tend to mark up even after a reasonable discount has been given to them. This practice frustrates the publishers' painstaking pricing exercise and may cause annoyance to governments and consumers as it encourages a situation in which the same publication may sell at different prices within the same country or even town.

In concluding this part of our discussion, let us look at pricing within a social framework. In most African countries, books are classified as essential commodities since they are considered vital for the educational welfare of those countries—most of which have given a lot of attention to educating their own people, something that was ignored during the years of colonial subjugation. But, in practice, books are far less essential to the African man than shelter, health, food, etc., which are basic for survival. Because of the high degree of illiteracy, and the multiplicity of local and foreign languages, the low development of reading habits, and the general increases in the cost of living that came in the wake of the oil boom of the early to mid 1970s, fewer and fewer books are being printed, fewer and fewer are being bought, creating an vicious circle and complicating the African publishers' pricing problems. This is a problem that will be with us for some time, until the standard of living for Africans improves.

SOME CONCLUDING REMARKS

I shall here make a few observations that will help us to discuss this whole issue of pricing publications.

I would discourage subsidies as a method of helping a publisher out of his pricing problems. Subsidies are given in certain social, economic, cultural, or political situations and may not always be available if those conditions are not there, and this might be at a time when you wish to reprint your book. This would compel you to almost double or treble the selling price of your book in the absence of a repeat of the original subsidy.

Printers will tend to encourage you to print more copies so that you can achieve a lower unit cost. I would advise you to resist this temptation as it is likely to lead to increased stock levels, storage problems, high insurance costs, depreciation, etc.

I would advise against use of half-tones and color work, except when these cannot be avoided—as, say, on the cover of a thriller. Color work costs a lot of money, and I do not think Africa is yet ready for this luxury.

Illustrations are part and parcel of a publication. Most contracts provide that the author should meet the cost of illustrations. It would be a good idea to approach this issue cautiously and perhaps spread the cost of illustrations out over possible future reprints so as to save your author the burden of paying for this and having to delay his royalty earnings until you recover those costs.

Advertising—some publishers look at advertising as a means of paying for or reducing their costs. Too much advertising tends to dilute the seriousness of a book, and I would recommend that in the case of journals, advertising should be restricted to 25 percent of content or less. Serious educational books should not carry advertising as this tends to compromise the quality and purpose of a book.

There is greater virtue in offering low royalties and low discounts, so as to price your books at affordable levels rather than trying to impress your authors and distributors with good terms at the expense of your reader.

Not every book you come across should be considered as a profit center. A good publisher's list should be properly balanced, with fast-selling books, midterm, income-earning publications, and long-term projects to cushion you for the future. It is not so much the strength of your bottom line but the contribution that you make to the academic and cultural welfare of your society that will be remembered.

Appendix
Recommended Pricing Schedule (assuming a U.S.$5 book)

	50% gross margin	55% gross margin
Selling price	$5.00	$5.00
less trade discount—25%	$1.25	$1.25
Receipts	$3.75	$3.75
less royalty (on the published price)—10%	$0.50	$0.50
	$3.25	$3.25
less production cost	$1.37	$1.19
Gross margin	$1.88	$2.06

You can ask your accountant to draw up a pricing schedule based on this formula, showing various unit costs and the resultant selling prices. Note that royalty and trade discount may vary depending on your contract with the author, and the terms agreed with your bookseller. For example, below is another pricing schedule for the same U.S.$5 book but assuming a trade discount of 20 percent and a royalty of 12.5 percent on receipts.

	50% gross margin	55% gross margin
Selling price	$5.00	$5.00
less trade discount—20%	$1.00	$1.00
Receipts	$4.00	$4.00
less royalty (on the published price)—12.5%	$0.50	$0.50
	$3.50	$3.50
less production cost	$1.50	$1.30
Gross margin	$2.00	$2.20

Notes

Chapter 1: "Kenyan Publishing: Independence and Dependence"

1. See Charles Richards' interview with Keith Smith in *African Book Publishing Record* 2 (July 1976): 161–64.

2. J. W. Chege, *Copyright Law and Publishing in Kenya* (Nairobi: East African Literature Bureau, 1978), 130–31.

3. John Nottingham, "Establishing an African Publishing Industry: A Study in Decolonisation," *Africa Affairs* 68 (April 1969): 139–44.

4. Henry Chakava, *Books and Reading in Kenya* (Paris: UNESCO, 1983).

5. See paper by John Ndegwa in *The Role of Books in Development: Proceedings of the Fifth Biennial Conference of the East African Library Association*, ed. J. Abukutsa (Nairobi: Kenya Library Association, 1974), 47.

6. Peter J. Gachathi, *Report on the National Committee on Education Objectives and Policies* (Nairobi: Government Printer, 1976), 123–25.

7. James Mwangi Kamunge, *Report on the Presidential Working Party on Education and Manpower Training for the Next Decade and Beyond* (Nairobi: Government Printer, 1988), 144.

8. Ibid., 81.

9. S. H. Ominde, *Kenya Education Commission Report* (Nairobi: Government Printer, 1964), 60.

10. Ibid., 60–61.

11. *Daily Nation*, 18 November 1985.

12. Ibid.

13. Canute P. M. Khamala, "A Survey of Reading Habits among Nairobi Primary and Lower Secondary School Children: Foundation for a National Book Policy in Kenya" (Nairobi: Kenya National Academy for Advancement of Arts and Sciences, 1980), 6 and Table 7.

Chapter 5: "International Copyright and Africa: The Unequal Exchange"

1. This is an Ndebele word that means a "meeting," usually one called to reconcile groups or sort out differences.

2. The majority of readers find the book difficult and slow to read and not offering much entertainment value compared to other knowledge distribution technologies.

3. This information is contained in the working paper of a WIPO Regional Seminar on Copyright and Neighboring Rights for African Countries, held in Nairobi, in July 1994.

4. For more details, see bibliography at end of essay.

5. Ibid., note 3 above.

6. For more details, see bibliography at end of essay.

7. See Eamon T. Fennessy, "US Copyright Expert Goes to Nigeria and Is Impressed," *Logos* 4, no.3 (1993): 159–61.

8. See chapter 1 of his *Book Publishing in a Societal Context: Japan and the West* (Tokyo: Japan Scientific Societies Press, 1990).

9. This was a copyright case between Evans Brothers (U.K.) and Heinemann Kenya Ltd. (presently known as East African Educational Publishers Ltd.) over a local edition, published by the latter, of Mohammed Said Abdalla's Kiswahili novel, *Kisima cha Giningi*.

10. Kiswahili is a Kenyan language spoken by most peoples of East and Central Africa.

11. Mr. Justice Frank Shields, formerly Judge, High Court of Kenya.

12. Their full address is: James Currey Publishers, 54b Thornhill Square, Islington, London, NI 1BE, U.K.

13. This information was made available to the writer by John-Willy Rudolph, executive director of KOPINOR, Norway, during a recent visit to that country.

14. Ibid., this provision in international copyright was also explained to the writer by KOPINOR.

Chapter 6: "Reading in Africa—Some Obstacles"

1. UNESCO, *Statistical Yearbook* 1980 (Paris: UNESCO, 1981), 905–06.

2. UNESCO, *An International Survey of Book Production During the Last Decades*: Statistical Reports and Studies, no. 26 (Paris: UNESCO, 1982).

3. Amu Djoleto, "Publishing in Ghana: Aspects of Knowledge and Development," in *Publishing in the Third World: Knowledge and Development*, ed. Philip G. Altbach, Amadio A. Arboleda, and S. Gopinathan (Portsmouth, N.H.: Heinemann, 1985, 76–86.

4. Modupe Oduyoye: "The Role of Chrisitan Publishing Houses in Africa Today" in *Publishing in African in the Seventies*, ed. Edwina Oluwasanui et al. (Ile-Ife, University of Ife Press, 1975).

5. Eva M. Rathgeber: "The Book Industry in Africa, 1973–1983 A Decade of Development?" in *Publishing in the Third World: Knowledge and Development*, ed. Altbach, Arboleda, and Gopinathan, 57–75.

6. Okot p'Bitek, *Song of Lawino and Ocol* (Nairobi: East African Publishing House, 1966), 183–91).

7. "A Survey of Reading Habits and Preferences among Nairobi Primary and Lower Secondary School Children", paper prepared by the Kenya National Academy for Advancement of Arts and Sciences, May 1980.

8. R. C. Staiger, *Roads to Reading* (Paris: UNESCO, 1979).

9. R. C. Staiger and C. Casey, *Planning and Organising Reading Campaigns: A Guide for Developing Countries* (Paris: UNESCO, 1983).

10. UNESCO - *Statistical Yearbook 1980:* "Newsprint, Printing Paper, and Writing Paper: Production, Imports, Exports and Consumption" (Paris: UNESCO, 1983), Table 8.9.

Appendix 1

An Indigenous African Book Publishing Industry: In Search of a New Beginning

Since independence, African governments have pursued policies aimed at book provision but have not paid attention to the more critical question of book creation and the critical role played by the publishers in this process. Because African governments have overlooked the publisher they have adopted simplistic strategies on an issue at the center of a nation's cultural integrity, an indigenous publishing industry.

Nigeria and Kenya, for example, at independence, had a thriving publishing industry, largely in the hands of the local branches of multinational firms. The authorities saw nothing wrong with this arrangement, as long as the books kept flowing and schools could afford to buy them. It took Gen. Murtala Mohammed's decree of 1973 for Nigerians to gain equity participation in some of these companies. In Kenya, the original arrangements are still in place although market forces have compelled two of the leading multinationals, Heinemann and Longman, to sell all or part of their equity.

Other countries such as Ghana, Uganda, and Tanzania had no publishing industries of their own at independence. They set up state publishing companies and entered into exclusive copublication arrangements with Macmillan publishing of the United Kingdom. These partnerships were of little benefit to the host countries, and were terminated within the first ten years of their taking effect. These countries, along with Zambia, which had not gone through the Macmillan stage, thereafter continued to depend on their parastatals for book supply until they were no longer able to perform this role.

Another mistake that African governments made was to dissolve their regional examining boards. If all West African English-speaking countries had continued with a common curriculum, a small country

From *African Publishing Review* (1993).

like Sierra Leone, for example, would now be importing its book needs from Ghana or Nigeria, and would not have to subject itself to foreign books and foreign examinations as at present.

Zimbabwe and Namibia, which got their independence much later, represent a more hopeful case study. In Zimbabwe, foreign publishers were allowed into the country on condition that local people were allowed to own a majority of the equity in their companies. In Namibia, a much smaller market, foreign publishers can only get their books into that country through local publishers. It is too early to assess the impact that the restriction of foreigners will have on Namibia's publishing industry. But in the case of Zimbabwe, this has been very successful, and the country has been able to build a strong local industry within the short period since independence.

In sum, approximately thirty years after independence, there is no African country that can claim to have indigenized its publishing industry. Nigerian and Zimbabwean companies might be majority owned, but the bulk of what they sell is imported or licensed from foreign publishers. The Kenyan publishing situation is currently complicated by the recent introduction of state publishing monopolies, and it will be some time yet before the whole industry passes into the hands of local people.

In South Africa, the local big boys are putting on their more acceptable face and proclaiming their readiness to serve a new South Africa. As for the foreign ones, Macmillan is already flirting with the African National Congress! What does this portend for the small independent publishers who supported the blacks during apartheid? Elsewhere on the continent, very little is happening. Even British publishers have discovered that it is easier to employ a lobby at the World Bank in Washington than to undertake hazardous promotional visits into Africa. How can we create an indigenous African publishing industry, capable of supplying the domestic market, as well as competing in World Bank book schemes for Africa, which are so frequent nowadays, and which are entirely dominated by foreign publishers? Nothing short of a new beginning can make this possible.

A new beginning is one that can apply the knowledge and experiences gathered over the years to a world now under the grip of tight monetarist policies. The African governments themselves must take the lead. A first step would be the formulation of national publishing or book policies. Many African countries do not have such policies, and this has made it difficult for their publishing industries to work in tandem with government. A sound and enlightened government policy should seek to empower the African publisher to take charge of this industry. Government policy should tackle key issues such as ownership, manpower, capital, manufacturing, distribution, and marketing. Below are various suggestions as to how these key areas may be approached in a new beginning.

OWNERSHIP

Firstly, the industry has to be wrested away from foreign publishers and state parastatals. Foreign publishers should no longer be allowed to operate freely in the African marketplace. They should be compelled under law to enter into partnerships with local publishers and encouraged to participate in the transfer of expertise to these people. It is not surprising that the two African countries with the most successful local industries, Nigeria and Zimbabwe, had introduced this legal requirement. Unless foreign publishers are forced to invest part of their capital and expertise locally, they will continue to exploit our markets from the metropolis, and we shall continue to be consumers rather than creators of books.

Secondly, the state must step out of publishing and must dismantle all its publishing monopolies. Publishing is a delicate and highly complicated operation, bringing together people of diverse skills and expectations. Each new book is unique, and needs to be handled differently. A publisher who has 500 titles in print is managing 500 product lines and taking more decisions on each than a businessperson who runs a company 500 times larger! Indeed, publishing is a very personalized trade that thrives best in the hands of an individual or group of individuals, as examples such as Longman, Macmillan, and Heinemann confirm. Because of the foregoing, it is not possible to expect a civil servant, however efficient, to run such a hands-on business.

If it is decided to sell the parastatals as a going concern, there should be no problem in finding buyers from among the staff, or other members of the public. If they are simply dissolved, local publishers can be given an opportunity to bid for whatever materials they may wish to continue publishing in return for a flat fee or a negotiated royalty.

The disappearance of parastatals would level the ground. There would be no monopolies and no government subsidies to distort market realities. A government without parastatals to fall back on would find it necessary to work more closely with industry on future donor schemes involving the World Bank and other lending agencies.

Manpower

For a publishing industry to succeed, it requires trained managers, editors, readers, artists, designers, illustrators, etc. It also requires the services of trained writers, printers, booksellers, and librarians in getting books to the users. The last twenty years have produced a number of trained people in these fields, some of whom are employed by the multinationals and in state parastatals. The majority are underemployed in small, cash-starved indigenous presses, while others have used the knowledge gained to acquire related employment, but outside the industry. We should encourage those people to come back and participate in the ownership of the new industry, which will this time enjoy the patronage of government. A study carried out last year on behalf of the African Publishers' Network (APNET) revealed that Africa has adequate training capacity, only that the courses lack coordination, are not well publicized, and are in need of standard certification. APNET, through the African Publishing Institute, will shortly be embarking on various regional and Africa-wide training programs. It is, therefore, unlikely that there will be a shortage of trained manpower, seeing the range of courses now in the offing. Moreover, the training issue should not be overemphasized. The publishing industry is a capital-intensive rather than labor-intensive venture and each company would require only a few well-trained people to produce many books.

Capital

As a business, publishing is unique and risky. A book can take up to two years to come out, from commissioning to finished copies, accumulating huge expenses along the way. Publishers entering the market for the first time would need to launch at least five books to make an impact. Then they might have to engage in promoting and publicizing the book before they can realize any sales. If the sales do come, usually via bookshops, they would be expected to give long credits, of up to 90 to 120 days. Of these first five titles, perhaps only three would succeed, while the other two would be "slow-sellers." One needs a lot of money to venture into publishing. Indigenous publishers have failed so far, largely because they have not had the money and have received no assistance from banks or any other sources during their critical stage of building a list.

Some years ago, the Dag Hammarskjold Foundation launched a loan-guarantee scheme for indigenous publishing in Kenya, with the prime aim of showing local banks that publishing is and can be profitable in the long run if properly capitalized and managed. African governments must now step in to provide their indigenous publishing firms with the kind of security that the foundation is giving the Kenyans. If they remember the amount of money they have invested in importing books all these years and the kinds of subsidy they are giving to their publishing parastatals, this should not be considered too much of a sacrifice. In fact, we would suggest that they should not only offer security but should also negotiate, on behalf of the publishers, at least a two-year moratorium on the loans and a reduced rate of interest for the first five years.

Another way of assisting local publishers is to grant them access to curriculum materials currently being published by government parastatals and open up the school textbook market to them. Revenue derived from the sale of textbooks will give them a firm foundation and enable them to invest in other essential but nontextbook areas. African governments should also play the role of coordinating and facilitating the needs of the industry by maintaining links between donors and publishers in the search for machinery, raw materials, and imported inputs necessary for book production.

MANUFACTURING

Some countries (e.g., Kenya, Nigeria, and Zimbabwe) have sufficient printing capacity within their private and public sectors. Kenya, for example, has excess capacity that should be able to export to neighboring countries. Raw materials such as paper, boards, inks, films, plates, etc. are produced in only a few places, and the bulk of these have to be imported from outside the continent. Our new policy here should be to import machinery and raw materials with a view to carrying out all our printing within Africa as much as possible. Most African countries do not impose any taxes on imported books, a good thing in itself, and yet impose heavy taxes on printing machinery and raw materials. Such duties would have to be lifted and printers granted loans and the foreign exchange to import machinery and spare parts. The important thing here is to get good, fast, and efficient service at a reasonable price.

DISTRIBUTION

Many African publishers have complained that they are unable to get their books to places where the would-be buyer can see them. They say there are far too few bookshops and libraries in Africa. The road and rail network is inadequate and some places are impossible to reach. They complain that the postal service is slow, expensive, and unreliable. Other methods of communication, such as telephone, telex, and fax do not work and are frustratingly time-consuming. How, then, can one effectively distribute books against these odds?

Firstly, we have to accept that Africa is an underdeveloped continent and it will take many years before these communication infrastructures are in place. But is it possible to communicate with each other within our regions and we can, for a start, limit our distribution activities within these regions. Services such as those provided by the African Books Collective will enable us to trade with each other across regions, albeit via Oxford, England, until some of these obstacles are overcome.

Secondly, some distribution problems are caused by bad government policies. For example, in Kenya, between the late 1970s and the early 1980s the Kenyan government took it upon itself to be the sole distributor of primary school textbooks. It was just planning to extend these services to secondary schools when, suddenly, it discontinued the practice. By this time, only 200 out of the original 300 booksellers were still in business. Today, since liberalization nine years ago, the number of booksellers has nearly trebled, and book distribution has become a lot more efficient! In the new beginning, African governments would have to pursue policies that encourage the widest distribution of books, by supporting booksellers.

Market

The book user constitutes the publishers' market. This market is adversely affected by diminishing national budgets, constantly changing curricula, and small home markets that are characterized by declining purchasing power. Our new policy would have to address these and all other means of expanding the market to books.

African governments have paid very little attention to adult education. More then one half of the continent is illiterate, and our new policy must include a program for the eradication of illiteracy on the continent. We can learn from the Tanzanians, whose literacy campaigns in the 1970s were so successful that a literacy rate of nearly 90 percent was achieved. Local publishers should be able to expand their market into this area by producing the literacy materials as well as the follow-up reading books, in order to minimize the danger of a lapse back into illiteracy as is the case in Tanzania.

Finally, it is incumbent upon African governments to provide their people with a congenial reading environment that can enable them to develop and practice reading habits. More school and public libraries should be built, and booksellers encouraged to set up in rural areas. Higher wages and better housing, coupled with rural electrification, would increase reading opportunities. A good publisher would serve both as the agent and the cure, identifying the interests of these new literates and providing them with relevant reading materials.

This paper has been addressed largely to African governments and their policymakers. This is because Africa's current publishing problems are a result of bad or misinformed policies adopted thirty years ago at independence and that for some reason have not been revised. This paper calls for a new beginning with more aggressive policies born out of our experiences and past failures. It emphasizes that only governments can take the African publishing industry out of the mess it is in now by placing the industry firmly in the hands of local publishers.

Appendix 2

Publishing and State Censorship in Kenya

Kenya boasts the largest and fastest-growing publishing industry in East Africa. If this growth is to continue, a number of important issues need to be addressed. Firstly, the industry lacks a policy or a set of policies that can define and guide its development path. Secondly, it suffers from shortage of capital investment at every level of operation. Thirdly, an underdeveloped market poses special production, marketing, and distribution problems. Finally, state intervention has tended to stifle the spirit of entrepreneurship and creativity. This essay will briefly discuss the first three problems, before taking a detailed look at state censorship in its various manifestations, from the overt to the covert.

The Kenyan publishing industry survives without the support of national statutes that, if in place, would have protected and helped guide and shape its direction. The industry suffers from a lack of a clear-cut national language policy, so that publishers are compelled to publish unprofitably in any of the three language categories—English, Kiswahili, and mother tongues. Furthermore, the country does not have an information policy, a publishing policy, or a book policy, although attempts in these directions have been made. Efforts to set up a national book development council have been unsuccessful so far. There are a lot of contradictions and grey areas in the industry, including the vexatious area of taxation. It is not surprising, therefore, that the Kenyan government has liberalized book imports on the one hand while pursuing state monopoly on the other.

Secondly, the industry suffers from acute shortage of capital. Banks will not lend to it because they consider it risky, and usually do not accept stocks as collateral. As a result of this, Kenyan publishers tend to restrict their publishing activity to the "safe" areas—textbooks and revision books—and tend to shy away from any long-term investments in areas such as fiction, academic, or reference publishing. The result is

---

From *Index on Censorship* (forthcoming 1996).

too much duplication in some areas and scarcity in the areas perceived to be risky. Lack of funds also undermines the quality of their product, as they resort to cheaper materials and untrained and inexperienced staff. Of greater relevance to our topic are those books that never get published because the publisher has no funds to invest in them. This problem affects all those involved in the book chain, perhaps the only exception being printers. Bookshops, libraries, and schools are all starved for cash, and because of this, authors do not make much money out of writing.

Poverty remains the greatest obstacle to book consumption in Kenya. The country has a per capita GNP of only U.S.$300, one of the lowest in the world. Problems of unemployment, food, health, and housing take priority over everything else. Education is perceived only in terms of paying school fees, and most Kenyans have yet to accept books as an integral part of the education process. Another worrying factor is that nearly 50 percent of the country is illiterate and therefore has no need for books. Of the remaining, only a small percentage has any disposable income and lacks any book reading or book buying habits. In fact, 80 percent of Kenya's population lives in rural areas with no access to all-weather roads, postal services, or electricity. Promoting and distributing books under such conditions are arduous tasks indeed.

State Censorship in Kenya

The Kenyan government exercises censorship of the print media by means of statutes ranging from its own constitution, the penal code, the Books and Newspapers Act, the Official Secrets Acts, the Films Stage Plays Act, and the Defamation Act. Acting through the minister responsible, the government can invoke any of these laws to ban a publication. Among the local publications so banned are *Kenya: Return to Reason*, by Kenneth Matiba, and the following journals and magazines—*Voice of Africa, Beyond, Financial Review, Development Agenda,* and *Inooro* (a Gikuyu newsmagazine previously published by the Catholic Diocese of Murang'a).

The list of banned foreign publications numbers around twenty, and includes such books as Salman Rushdie's *Satanic Verses, The Quotations of Chairman Mao Tse-tung,* William Attwoods's *The Reds and the*

Blacks; and periodicals such as *Who Rules Kenya?, Revolution in Africa, The African Communist,* and *Sauti ya Wanachi,* (Voice of the people), to mention only a few. A ban on a periodical would normally affect all past and future issues. Foreign newspapers or magazines containing an unsavory story about Kenya have been seized at the airport and destroyed or confiscated for several days.

For a country of Kenya's reputation, this list is indeed modest. However, a look at the events of the last ten years points to a systematic attempt to stifle creativity. Several writers have left the country after being jailed, detained, or harassed, to live and work abroad. These include Ngugi wa Thiong'o (about whom more later), Abdilatif Abdalla, Ali Mazrui, Alamin Mazrui, Maina wa Kinyatti, Micere Mugo, Kimani Gecau, Ngugi wa Mirii, and Atieno Odhiambo. Local and foreign journalists have been arrested and/or beaten up in the course of their professional work. Publishers' offices have been raided and vandalized, while printers such as Fotoform and Colourprint have had their machines immobilized and materials confiscated and destroyed. The writer has been visited by senior police officers on the prowl for manuscripts, proofs, or new publications. Dramatic performances have been denied license, or cancelled without cause. Between 1987 and 1993, the plays affected included *Kilio cha Haki (A cry for justice), Animal Farm, An Enemy of the People, Fate of a Cockroach, Drumbeats of Kirinyaga* (a musical), and *The Master and the Frauds.* Ironically, *Animal Farm* and *An Enemy of the People* were previously prescribed for study as secondary school examination texts.

The case of Ngugi deserves greater elaboration. He is Kenya's leading creative writer, and one with an international reputation. His novels and plays are constantly assigned for study in African schools, but no longer in Kenya. He was detained for one year in 1977 for his role in writing a play in his Gikuyu language, *Ngaahika Ndenda* (I will marry when I want) and staging it before large crowds at Kamiriithu, a local community center. This play was published soon after his release from detention, followed by two other books he had written while in prison—a memoir, *Detained: A Writer's Prison Diary,* and *Caitani Mutharaba-ini* (Devil on the cross), a novel. He was not allowed to resume his teaching duties at the University of Nairobi, in spite of repeated appeals for reinstatement. His ambitious musical play, *Maitu Njugira* (Mother, sing for me) was stopped while in rehearsal and just before it opened to the public. Frustrated and bitter, Ngugi left the country in 1982 and now lives in the United States, where he teaches literature at New York University. In 1988, *A Grain of Wheat* became the last of his books to be removed from the list of prescribed school texts in literature. His absence from the Kenyan literacy scene has seriously affected the country's creative atmosphere and has been a great disincentive to young writers. Readers of his books are stigmatized by the state, although none of the titles are officially banned.

We shall now look at the rather more subtle forms of censorship employed by the state. The Kenyan education curriculum is so packed that it does not allow any time for leisure reading. Consequently, students are now graduating from primary and secondary school without adequate exposure to fictional works. In fact, literature as a subject has all but disappeared from the school curriculum. It has been "integrated" into the English-language syllabus, and students are expected to study only one novel and one play for their secondary school examination—a far cry from the wide range of texts this subject used to attract. It is not surprising that the level of written and spoken language has fallen dramatically among the youth, and they are no longer able to express themselves properly.

The Kenya Schools Drama Festival is another case in point. During the 1970s, this festival used to feature some very original plays, usually written by the students themselves. They would tackle such issues as corruption, greed, road carnage, social inequality, cruelty to women and children etc., taking a critical view of these and other ills in our society. Then, in the 1980s, the government banned what it called "political plays" from the festival, and advised education officers to censor any plays with political messages likely to divide the people. All plays were to project the country in a positive light, promote development, and interpret the president's motto of "love, peace and unity." Although the festival continues, it has lost much of its creative sparkle and spice.

This same creative lethargy in schools can also be seen at universities and within society in general. The university institution has been largely politicized, and a majority of university professors absorbed into the state system. Creativity is stifled through curtailment of literary seminars, journals, and writers' workshops, and a general lack of facilities or incentives to promote and reward academic excellence. There is a lack of an intellectual atmosphere and debate on important issues of the day.

Society at large does not respect or reward creative talent, and writers rarely feature on National Honours lists. There is no scheme by which talent is spotted or nurtured. Support for community recreation centers, theater groups, libraries, and other artistic activities is lacking. There are no policies or laws that can provide a framework for the creation of such institutions in the future. From the local community through to schools and the highest institutions of learning to professional societies and clubs, not enough attention is being given to the arts. As one would expect, a creative environment cannot emerge in a society characterized by fear and silence.

The creation of state publishing institutions represent another subtle form of state censorship. The two state publishers, Kenya Literature Bureau and Jomo Kenyatta Foundation, are the only ones allowed to publish textbooks for the Kenyan school system. Commercial publishers are not barred from publishing textbooks but, if found acceptable, they can only be used as supplementary or reference material. With this one stroke, the state is not only able to control the content of what is taught in schools, but is able to keep commercial publishers sufficiently weakened and without funds to invest in risky areas like fiction. State involvement in publishing not only leads to a lowering of standards by discouraging competition but also provides a tool that the state employs to censor commercially published books.

CONCLUSION

It should be appreciated that although state censorship manifests itself in all sorts of ways in Kenya, it is not the most significant factor denying Kenyans access to books. A discussion of this topic has to be held within the context of other even more pressing problems confronting the Kenyan book publishing industry today. As we pointed out at the start, these problems include poverty, illiteracy, and an undeveloped book marketing and distribution infrastructure, coupled with a lack of book buying and book reading habits. Publishing in Kenya will continue to remain a minority concern until these issues are tackled. But a government capable of tackling these problems must first have the will and insight to remove outdated laws from its statutes, and promulgate new ones, and be in a position to guarantee certain basic human rights. On this score, the censorship issue becomes as important as any other.

Appendix 3

Reading Promotion in South Saharan Africa

I would like to thank the International Publishers Association's Reading Committee for giving me the honor and privilege of addressing you on this important subject. Nearly ten years ago, I was similarly honored to address a plenary session of an International Federation of Library Associations (IFLA) conference on this very topic. In that address, which was subsequently published in their journal (*IFLA* no. 4, 1984), I dwelt at length on obstacles to reading in Africa, concluding that its quality and quantity could only be improved if the continent's poverty and low living standards were tackled. I pleaded with African governments to pay attention to this matter, and called upon the rest of the world and its relevant institutions to assist. Today, I shall employ a different approach, although it may lead me to the same conclusion.

UNESCO's 1992 *Statistical Yearbook* contains depressing statistics about the reading (or lack of reading) situation in Africa (1990). The continent, with more than 12 percent of the world's population, produced only 1.2 percent of its books, compared to Europe (52.4 percent), Asia (26.7 percent), and North America (12.6 percent). The situation was no different with newspapers, with Africa producing and/or distributing 1.0% of the world's newspapers, as opposed to Europe (44.5%), Asia (33.3%) and North America (11.6%). The information on illiteracy is difficult to summarize because it is given by country and covers different periods, but it does not take too much looking to see that more than half of the continent's population is illiterate, women being worse off then their male counterparts.

To help us understand the present state of reading in Africa, we shall look at the historical, sociocultural, educational, and economic factors that have helped to shape it. Later, we shall see what achievements have been made so far. We shall conclude by highlighting what

---

Paper presented at the International Publishers Association conference, Frankfurt, October 9, 1993.

remains to be done and what external assistance may be needed to support initiatives for the promotion of books and reading in Africa south of the Sahara.

HISTORICAL FACTORS

Reading has a relatively short history in Africa. It was introduced into mainland Africa by missionaries only in the last century. It seems to have acquired a negative image in the minds of Africans right from the beginning. They were suspicious of it and of the men who had brought it, and the manner in which it was introduced to them. Young people were literally dragged to "schools" and forcibly taught how to read and write in a way that bore no resemblance to their traditional forms of education. In order to persuade these people to stay in school, the missionaries tended to overemphasize the benefits and privileges the "reading" would bestow upon those who mastered it. It would make them different people—*wazungus* (white men), with access to a good job, money, and a comfortable life. Thus, from the outset, Africans began to see reading (for that was what education was called) only in utilitarian terms; they would read, and do away with the practice as soon as they acquired the promised benefits.

This attitude, in my view, has been partly responsible for the very slow development of reading habits in Africa. Africans understand the value of reading to pass their examinations or to gain promotion in their jobs. Once that has been achieved, only very few continue to read beyond the daily newspaper or magazine. Fortunately, the situation is better than it was ten years ago, and is improving steadily especially with young people, the majority of whom are now taking up reading as a hobby.

Before we leave the historical factors and the role played by missionaries, it should be pointed out that they also pioneered printing and publishing on the continent. They transcribed African languages, gave them an alphabet, and translated the bible, hymn books, and bible stories into those languages. Later, they were able to publish some African stories, which proved quite popular. But generally, Africans were not consulted about what kinds of books they wanted to read. They gradually accepted reading as an unpleasant duty to be endured and disposed of when they left school.

Sociocultural Factors

I am on record elsewhere as having observed that reading is alien to African culture, by the very fact that it is an individual and private act. Africans tend to live a communal lifestyle in which each member gives as much as he takes. Reading has no place against other creative and recreative activities such as talking, dancing, singing, drama, sports, etc. This, combined with the fact that the books currently on the market do not strike a deep familiar cord in the hearts and minds of African readers, has made it difficult for reading to take root. These books deal largely with situations and settings that have little meaning or relevance to the reader's life. It has been observed that in Africa reading is an alienating process—so that the more one reads, the more one loses one's roots. To correct this impression, it would be necessary, not only to provide the African reader with relevant and useful reading materials, but also to explore more deeply into the possibility of publishing more in local languages. Currently, the majority of the reading materials available to the African child and adult are foreign.

Educational Factors

The problems created by missionaries still exist in Africa's educational system today. In most countries, the curriculum is so crowded that there is no time left for anything else. The emphasis seems to be only on passing examinations, so that subjects like reading are sidelined. Little or no emphasis is given to the establishment of public and school libraries, and the little money available is used to buy textbooks.

African governments have adopted policies that do not favor reading. For example, in the critical area of language policy, one finds no policy statements, only vague pronouncements that do not amount to much. It is strange that African countries have chosen, uncritically, to retain the languages of their erstwhile colonial masters as their official languages, even when these languages are accessible to only a small percentage of their populations. And without a proper language policy, they cannot address the critical issue of illiteracy, as it would be more cost-effective to launch literacy programs in only a few local languages rather than in the more than 1,200 reportedly in use. A language policy would have to be in place first if selection of the languages to be developed is to have any meaning.

On the whole, African governments have not pursued enlightened book policies. They have done little to support local publishing industries, and have continued to levy duty on imported books and book production inputs. The book loans they have received from the World Bank and other donors have largely been spent on importing books instead of creating or supporting local publishing industries. The World Bank itself has been hoodwinked into supporting schemes that are inimical to its own declared policy of building local capacities within the private sector, and continues to work with multinationals and national governments to the detriment of local industries.

ECONOMIC FACTORS

Of all the factors that hinder reading and reading promotion, economic factors are the most important. Africa abounds with poverty, war, and famine. Most countries are unable to meet their recurrent costs of education, let alone the development costs that include books and other teaching materials. They are unable to provide education to all their children—to afford to introduce compulsory universal primary education. Many children do not, therefore, have the opportunity of even going to school. African countries cannot afford to build enough libraries, whether public or school, and stock them adequately. They do not have a transportation network developed enough to get books into the rural areas, or from one country into another. They suffer from inadequate and/or unsuitable housing, so that many people live in crowded conditions not suited to reading. Moreover, most rural areas lack the basic facilities, including electricity. In short, a reading environment does not exist, and considerable investment would be necessary before a reading infrastructure could be created.

Although we have mentioned above that Africans are reluctant readers, we must emphasize that part of the reason for this is not just cultural but also economic. In various studies carried out in Africa, it has been proved that every book or newspaper bought is read by at least ten more people. While this demonstrates my African communalism point, it should also caution against the tendency to calculate readership levels by using statistics of bookshop sales and library borrowings. This point emphasizes the fact that a large majority of those wanting to read cannot afford to buy a book. Unfortunately, book prices are continually rising as the value of African currencies fails to hold against international currencies.

The UNESCO *Statistical Yearbook* shows that the number of titles published in Africa increased from 7,000 in 1965 to 12,000 in 1980. The figure increased to 13,000 titles by 1985 and has remained the same since. The slowing down in African book output during the last ten years must be of some concern to all, and to African governments in particular. Unfortunately, the statistics for imports show that over the same period the level of the continent's book imports dropped substantially in a majority of countries. So, generally speaking, fewer Africans have access to books in the 1990s than in the 1980s.

The same statistics show that the number of schools has gone up and enrollment figures have increased both for males and females. Although public expenditure on education has increased in absolute terms, the amount spent per inhabitant has fallen from U.S.$42 in 1980 to U.S.$35 in 1990. These statistics should not lead us to conclude that the number of readers has dropped. It has been stated elsewhere in this paper that one book or newspaper in Africa is read by many others. The same is true of textbooks, and African governments now publicly admit that, on average, between six and eight children share each textbook. So, although the number of pupils and school libraries may have increased, individual holdings must have dropped substantially. All these facts paint a sad picture of the quality of education and of reading on the continent.

SOME ACHIEVEMENTS

In spite of the foregoing, Africa has made some achievements in the area of reading. There has been an increase in the number of readers both in and out of school, especially among the youth. The number of school, public and special libraries has increased, although, as we have noted above, their acquisitions have not increased in the last ten years. The availability of fiction from Heinemann's African Writers Series and Macmillan's Pacesetters has added local spice to Africans' reading menu. Of course, foreign exchange has not always been available to facilitate importation of these and other paperbacks by such popular writers as Harold Robbins, Danielle Steele, Stephen King, Robert Ludlum, Sidney Sheldon, Frederick Forsyth, David Bagely, Len Deighton, Jeffery Archer, Barbara Taylor Bradford, and Alastair Maclean—in addition, of course, to the old classics that continue to appeal to the more seasoned and habitual readers. At this point, one should acknowledge the role being played by the World Bank in extending loans to African countries for book purchase. Without these, some countries could have become bookless societies by now.

There is increasing publishing activity on the continent. More local publishers are setting up, even as international publishers continue to reduce the scale of their African operations. The need for professional associations at the national, regional, and even continental level is now being addressed. In many countries, authors, publishers, booksellers, printers, and librarians, etc., have formed book associations and in three countries—Ghana, Nigeria, and Zimbabwe—all these have come together to form a national book development council. With such a council, it is possible to work together within the industry and with the government in promoting the welfare of the book. The Bellagio Group of Donors should be complimented for assisting African publishers to set up the African Publishers' Network (APNET)—in a move that, it is hoped, will result in the formation of a continentwide publishers association. When that time comes, it will be possible for all African publishers to speak with one voice, something that is not possible today.

Book fairs are an important way of exposing the reading public to books. In the 1970s, Africa had only one book fair, based in Nigeria. Today, we have the Zimbabwe Book Fair, which has now acquired international stature, and other national fairs in Senegal, Nigeria, Kenya, Tanzania, and Zambia, etc. In fact, most countries nowadays have an annual book function of one sort or another. Other forms of book promotion are developing apace, with more book reviews appearing in newspapers, radio, and television, although this last medium has yet to be harnessed in the promotion of reading.

What Remains to be Done

Although some progress has been achieved, a lot more remains to be done to promote reading in Africa. For example, no systematic attempts have been made to conduct readership campaigns on a national or regional basis. Few countries teach reading education as a subject, and no courses exist to assist people to improve the quality and quantity of their reading. With the exception of Nigeria, which has a fully functional reading association, other countries do not have a forum through which they can expand their reading interests. It would be unrealistic to expect Africa to divert its meager resources into reading promotion when its mainstream educational programs are on the brink of collapse. We would, therefore, like to call upon all countries of the North, international agencies such as the World Bank, UNESCO, the International Publishers Association, IFLA, the International Reading Association, and the International Booksellers Federation, and others to do everything possible to assist Africa in its efforts to become a reading society.

In its book aid schemes for Africa the World Bank has emphasized book provision rather than book creation. We believe that the time has come when all efforts should be directed toward strengthening the African book publishing chain, as it is only through this approach that local capacity and self-sustainability can be created. Various studies have been made of the industry, and its needs are known. The African publishing industry should be freed from the patronage of national governments and the high-handed maneuvers of multinational publishers. The industry needs training, and this hopefully should become available when APNET launches its training programs, via the proposed African Publishers Institute. The industry is further starved financially, although this problem could be relieved if governments were persuaded to step out of publishing so that the lucrative educational market might be supplied by commercial publishers. Solving problems of book distribution, nationally and regionally, is a long-term undertaking, but a start will have been made if attention is given to the other points raised above.

CONCLUSION

In summary, we would like to emphasize that to increase reading in Africa, we should avoid crowding our curricula, develop school, class, and home libraries, and make suitable reading materials available to our reading public. For the rest of the population, we need to adopt a longer-term strategy, with a view to creating a reading environment that would sustain literacy and reading; in this way, the reading habit itself would evolve gradually as incomes rise and housing improves; in short, reading habits would develop concomitantly with the general raising of people's living standards. This whole effort requires financial, material, and human resources and will be difficult to achieve without assistance from the international community. Significant achievements have been made, but greater challenges lie ahead.

Once more, I thank the organizers for inviting me, and you for being such a good audience. Thank you.

Appendix 4

The World Bank and African Publishing

The World Bank has been involved in textbook provision schemes for Africa since 1963. It started modestly by providing funding for the purchase of off-the-shelf books. From the mid-1970s to the early 1980s, its involvement broadened to include the acquisition of raw materials and printing equipment. From the late 1980s, the Bank has found itself more deeply involved even in matters of textbook development, production, and distribution.

Currently, nearly 70 percent of the Bank's education projects, involving millions of dollars, have a textbook component. For example, in 1991, twenty-three out of thirty-three education projects in sub-Saharan Africa had a textbook component. Indeed, in that year, the Bank's budget for financing textbook purchases worldwide was a staggering U.S.$380.2 million.

The Bank's textbook provision policy has been guided by the need to respond promptly by putting appropriate books on children's desks in an effort to maintain and even improve the quality of education. More recently, it has commissioned book-sector studies as a means of determining the exact needs of recipient countries, before setting up a project. In almost all the cases, tenders have been advertised abroad and all the procurement sourced from there, and African countries have been mere recipients. All the book-sector studies have been carried out by foreigners, who have normally given a thorough and factual analysis of the situation but have always shied away from proposing long-term solutions, which, in any case, are outside the Bank's present policy framework.

African publishers have only recently become aware of the important role played by the World Bank in book supplies to the continent. They are critical of the Bank's policies, but they have not had a channel through which to ventilate their grievances. Many countries

---

From *African Publishing Review* (1994).

do not have publishers associations, and in cases where these exist, they are not strong enough to be heard. The founding of the African Publishers Network (APNET), in February 1992, has made it possible for African publishers to work together to find solutions to the many problems that beset their industry. Many changes have taken place in Africa in the last thirty years, and African publishers are producing books that are pedagogically and culturally correct. The World Bank's book policy has not been revised to enable it to take advantage of these developments and to source some of its requirements from within the continent itself. The Bank has continued to apply the same uniform policy over the years, even where the situation differs from one country to another.

In December 1993, a delegation of APNET officials visited the World Bank to acquaint itself with the Bank and explore ways in which they could participate in its book provision programs. After a series of meetings at which World Bank officials outlined in detail the policies, procedures, and regulations governing its textbook programs, the delegation felt that more attention should be given to a number of areas if African publishers were to benefit from these schemes:

TENDERING PROCEDURES

These operate on the assumption that Africa is the recipient, while the West is the supplier. Tenders are drawn and published in *Development Business*, a World Bank journal published in Switzerland. In most cases these tenders are not even published in the recipient countries. The delegation felt that the World Bank should, in addition to international competitive bidding, also consider local competitive bidding, or even direct contracting in order to source some of the books from within the region, or even the recipient country itself, where possible.

The delegation was pleasantly surprised to find that the Bank is now making a distinction between the pedagogical and industrial issues involved in book publishing. Instead of funding government institutes of education to undertake both, they are encouraging them to handle the pedagogical side only, so that the manufacturing aspect can be tendered for by printers and publishers. This is a step in the right direction.

The delegation recommended direct contracting in cases where books already exist and are already on the recommended list, since to follow tendering procedures in such cases would be counterproductive and time wasting. The Bank promised to consider this request but warned that it is wary of single sourcing. The delegation also suggested that giving money to school heads so that they can buy books of their choice might be more effective in some countries. This, too, will be considered. The Bank is in the process of revising its tendering procedures and is welcoming comments from all parties concerned. As these procedures are quite technical it was agreed that the Bank would make available funds to train publishers in these new procedures, once they come into force.

BUILDING LOCAL CAPACITY

The delegation's basic message to the World Bank was: "Don't give us fish. Teach us how to fish." It regretted the fact that although the World Bank was encouraging building local capacities and sustainability in all its other policies, this was not the case in textbook provision. The delegation argued strongly that if support was given to African publishing industries, these would flourish and Africa would become self-sufficient and the Bank would no longer need to respond to emergency appeals as it is doing and has from the beginning. Bank officials confirmed that these words "are like sweet music to our ears." However, they argued, the Bank's primary objective in this case is to respond to textbook scarcity in schools by "putting books on children's desks." Developing African publishing is not part of the Bank's objective.

This is the crux of the problem. APNET should take on the challenge of persuading the Bank to look at this problem from a mid- to longer-term view. Unfortunately, publishing development is uneven throughout the continent, and it would be foolhardy for some countries to claim that they can build their capacities sufficiently to become self-sustaining. But this is possible with others—such as Nigeria, Zimbabwe, Kenya, Ghana, Ethiopia, Tanzania, Zambia, and Uganda. The World Bank should be persuaded to change its present "emergency" approach and adopt a more far-sighted policy that can give the push required to enable publishing industries in these countries to take off.

BOOK-SECTOR STUDIES

It was noted that all the book-sector studies on African countries (nine, to date), which normally prepare the ground for subsequent book projects, were prepared by foreigners. Although the studies are factual and thorough in their analysis of country situations, they tend to have a blanket conclusion for all countries: namely, there is no capacity for fulfilling demand locally and therefore books have to be imported. The selection process itself is heavily influenced by foreign suppliers, and some textbooks are imported into the country even when more acceptable alternatives, both from a pedogogical and cultural point of view, are available locally.

The delegation recommended that African book professionals be invited to take part in such consultancies. The Bank accepted this proposal and will begin to build up a database of African advisers and researchers.

TRAINING

The issue of training permeated all our discussions, at every level and on every subject. We were able to tell the Bank about the African Publishers Institute and the kind of courses we plan to offer. This is an area that is receiving welcome support from international donors, and the Bank was asked to put its weight behind training African book professionals. This was accepted and a commitment given to fund a seminar on the Bank's procurement procedures, with support for other training schemes to follow.

THE BANK, GOVERNMENTS, AND THE PUBLISHING INDUSTRY

There is an awkward relationship between these three. The Bank made it clear that it lends only to governments and cannot, therefore, deal directly with African publishers. The delegation felt that support from the Bank could strengthen its hand in dealing with African governments. The industry could best tackle issues like state publishing monopolies, privatization and liberalization, use of donor funds, taxation, and other forms of state intervention, etc., if it knew it had the backing and support of the Bank and if the Bank were sending out similar signals. The delegation was informed that the Bank's power to influence governments is often overrated. While it can give suggestions and offer alternative ways of doing things, it cannot dictate to foreign governments. Finally, the need to work together in a triangular relationship was stressed, and a minimum program of cooperation agreed. There will be a regular exchange of information, ideas, documents, and project updates that will enable APNET to gain a deeper insight into the operations of the Bank than was possible hitherto.

After this meeting, the delegation met and agreed on the need to set up a World Bank Projects' Committee in order to maintain close contact and dialogue with the Bank. It is also important to maintain a link with the other major player, African governments, without whose cooperation any gains from World Bank connections might dissipate. In this vein, I would suggest that APNET establish contact with a political grouping, such as the Organisation of African Unity, through which it can work closely with African governments. With the cooperation and support of these two major players on the scene, African publishing could secure the financial backing and political goodwill that it so desperately needs in order to take off.

Appendix 5

The African Publishers' Network: An Overview

The seed that germinated, to become the African Publishers' Network (APNET), was planted at a conference in Bellagio, Italy, in February 1991. Organized by the Obor Foundation of the United States, the conference addressed itself to the publishing situation in the Third World, more specifically Africa and Asia. The presentations on Africa were particularly revealing. Nearly all the papers dealt with the "problems" and "challenges" facing African publishing. There was not a single success story. One paper had the title "Africa: The Neglected Continent." Another outlined what French publishers were doing for Africa, raising doubts about whether or not indigenous publishing existed in Francophone Africa. When it came to discussing World Bank book provision schemes, one African publisher wanted to know what he should do to qualify as a supplier to these tenders. Many more embarrassing questions were asked. It was clear that the World Bank and other international donor agencies knew very little about indigenous African publishing and vice versa.

This conference not only resulted in the publication of a book, *Publishing and Development in the Third World* (edited by Philip G. Altbach and published in Oxford by Hans Zell Publishers in 1991), which has helped to bridge this information gap; it also inspired a group of donors present, led by the Rockefeller Foundation, to hold subsequent meetings and to evolve themselves into the Bellagio Group of Donors to African Publishing. They further agreed to assist African publishers to form themselves into a counterpart group, whose vision they had helped to shape and with whom they hoped to work together for the welfare of the African publishing industry. A year later, in 1992, representatives from eleven African countries founded APNET in Harare, Zimbabwe. Today, the Network has members from more than 20 Afri-

---

From the *Development Directory of Indigenous Publishing*, ed. Carol Priestley (1995).

can countries, covering more than 1,000 publishers, with its mission essentially being the empowerment of the African publisher.

Indigenous African publishing has been neglected right from the beginning in the days of preindependence Africa. The colonial governments did not like it because they considered it to be subversive, agitative, and "Communist," and did all in their power to suppress it. They invited cosmopolitan publishers to publish for their colonies, so that by the 1950s and 1960s the African publishing industry was under the control of foreign multinationals. At independence, most African governments did not formulate or pursue policies that would empower the African publisher and equip him with the skills and financial capacity to enable him to compete with his multinational counterpart. Many responded to the multinational threat by creating state parastatals, which were very quickly run down through inefficiency, corruption, and bad management. Recent moves toward structural adjustment and market economies have posed a major threat both for the parastatal publishers and indigenous publishing, as none of them is strong enough to respond to these changes. The arrival of APNET could not have been more timely, coming as it did at the dawn of privatization and liberalization.

One may wonder why African publishers have for so long been isolated from the international book community. How was it that, as late as 1991, African publishers were unaware of the operations of the World Bank's book provision schemes for Africa, although these had been going on for the last 30 years? How was it that none of the African publishers who attended the Bellagio Conference had ever heard of *Development Business*, the journal in which the World Bank publishes its book tenders? Why, they wondered, couldn't the World Bank publish its tenders in our national newspapers if it expects a response from us?

The answer is that the rest of the world knows very little about African publishing. They see African publishing in terms of British, French, and Portuguese enterprises on the continent. The African publisher himself is financially weak and not aggressive or entrepreneurial enough to get his voice heard. His own government does not care, because its main concern is not to develop a publishing industry but to ensure that children get books on their desks, regardless of their origin or content. The World Bank shares the same view along with other bilateral donors and international agencies. Regular contact and exchanges with these groups should convince them of the need to adopt a holistic and longer-term strategy that would build local publishing capacities and guarantee sustainability.

Very little effort has been made to inform the rest of the world about African publishing and to enlist its support and cooperation. One individual whose efforts should be acknowledged here is Hans Zell. Since organizing the first African Book Fair in Ife, Nigeria, in 1973, Hans has been an institution in himself, promoting African publishing through his journal, the *African Book Publishing Record*, and through the many books, papers, and bibliographies he has written and/or published. He was the founding secretary of Africa's prime book prize, the Noma Award for publishing in Africa, a position that he still holds, and is a founder member of the African Books Collective, an external distribution outlet for African-published books, based in Oxford, England, to which he now serves as consultant.

UNESCO also played a creditable role. Its primary mission was to encourage African countries to set up book development councils, as they considered these the ideal vessel for planning and coordinating government and private-sector efforts in the field of publishing development. They had used this formula in Asia and South America with a measure of success. At a UNESCO-sponsored seminar in Accra in 1968, this idea was formally endorsed and delegates mandated to go and form such councils in their own countries. UNESCO continued to hold more meetings and seminars throughout the 1970s and early 1980s, urging African governments to spearhead the setting up of these councils. Today, there are only three fully functioning councils in Africa—namely, Ghana, Nigeria, and Zimbabwe. The reason for this bad track record is that UNESCO appears to have assumed that the thinking of government and industry was complementary on this issue. The reality was far from this. Most African publishers know that a council headed by a civil servant would not serve the interests of the industry, while, on the other hand, African governments would be suspicious of entrusting their education and information industries to the private sector. UNESCO had other interesting programs involving publishing children's books and translations and even helped in setting up a center in Yaoundé, Cameroon, to coordinate and promote these activities. Most African governments and their publishing industries have not yet convinced each other of the need to work together.

It is against this background that the founding of APNET must be seen vis-à-vis its mission and detailed programs of action. APNET is aware of the many problems besetting the African publisher: the lack of investment capital, the lack of training at all levels of publishing management, low readership levels compounded by lack of national, regional, and continental markets and distribution infrastructures. All these problems can only be tackled in an environment conducive to dialogue. APNET believes that African publishing can only advance if all the parties involved in the book trade—i.e., the industry, African governments, and foreign donors—can work together. To this end, it seeks to encourage the formation of national publishers' associations where they do not exist and to strengthen them where they exist. It seeks to work closely with African governments and to encourage them to formulate national publishing and book policies that favor the growth of local publishing industries. And, finally, it hopes to work closely with donors to African education and to help harmonize their programs and policies with those of the governments and the local publishing industries.

We shall not here expound on APNET's mission or program of action; rather we shall very briefly discuss what it has achieved in its first two years of existence in relation to its core programs. First of all, it must be accepted that APNET is an umbrella association of national publishers' associations. The need to establish contact with these associations and to provide them with a forum within which to communicate to us and with each other was of paramount importance. Our first task, therefore, was to start a newsletter, *African Publishing Review*, through which it has been possible to interact with fellow publishers from all over the continent in English, French, and Portuguese and with our donors and well-wishers abroad. This exercise has enabled us to build up a database of addresses and information not available before. Already the *Review's* wide circulation is creating awareness and sensitizing individuals and organizations as we learn from each other's experiences.

The other program we shall discuss briefly concerns the work of the African Publishing Institute (API). APNET has done more work here than is apparent. It has drafted a funding proposal that has been accepted by the donors and two training coordinators have been appointed. The East and Central African coordinator has put his program in motion, and the first courses started in May 1994. As recommended by the board, the courses to be given priority are "training trainers" and "short regional courses." Before we embarked on the training program, we carried out a survey to find out what kinds of courses were available on the continent. These turned out to be more numerous than expected, and it was thus agreed that, in some cases, API would be required to simply coordinate or standardize existing courses for purposes of certification. APNET recognizes that the lack of training at appropriate levels is one of the factors retarding publishing development on the continent.

The last program I will discuss here relates to the establishment of an African Publishing and Resources Center. APNET has been fortunate to secure from Hans Zell, free of charge, his entire archive on African publishing over the last 30 years. This archive is presently being classified and put on computer and will be shipped to APNET headquarters in Harare, where it will be housed. It is hoped that smaller resource centers will be developed in each region, and these may have to draw on the materials to be domiciled in Harare.

Our other successes over this short period include a buyers/sellers meeting in Mauritius in May 1993 when deals involving purchase of rights, printing, and finished copies, were negotiated and concluded, and new agency arrangements set up. In December 1993, an APNET delegation visited the World Bank in Washington for a series of meetings, the results of which are likely to influence the Bank's book provision policies for Africa.

Let us conclude by taking a look at the challenges that lie ahead for APNET. If it is able to sustain its present programs as outlined above, this in itself will be an achievement. However, its success will largely be measured by its ability to help improve the lot of the African indigenous publisher. To my mind, this means helping him to gain access to investment capital and secure a greater share of his home market and develop a capacity to tap the regional and African markets as a whole. This will be impossible unless, or until, APNET is able to forge a working relationship with African governments and international (donor) agencies, including the World Bank.

In short, APNET should establish itself as a "third force," in what should emerge as a triangular relationship between these agencies and African governments. The World Bank, for example, believes in building local capacities for sustainable development and yet applies emergency measures in its book provision policies for Africa. Continued dialogue can help bring about a change of heart, to get the Bank to support longer-term projects developed locally in place of the present policy of responding to immediate needs by placing books on the desks of African school children. Also, by drawing worldwide attention to the plight of African publishers, APNET may be able to attract bilateral aid, such as the cooperation existing between Finland and Zambia today. Influencing African governments is likely to be more difficult, but less so in the present mood of privatization and liberalization. APNET should take it upon itself to persuade African governments to formulate national publishing or book policies that should govern the industry in this critical area of national development. These policies would not only cover the role to be played by local publishers and national publishers' associations, but should come out with proposals on how they can be helped to face competition in the marketplace, especially from multinationals. The Zimbabwe government's policy requiring multinationals to set up in equity partnership with local people has had a positive impact on that country's book industry. African governments would have to consider all these factors and other policies that would be instrumental in bringing about a regional or an African common market for books. To be able to talk to African governments, APNET would need strong national associations and would endeavor to set such bodies up, where none exist. Indeed, APNET itself would eventually have to drop the word "Network" and transform itself into a bona fide association of national publishers associations so as to enhance its credibility as a serious counterpart organization that can work hand-in-hand with African governments.

There are many things that APNET is doing, has done, or will do that are not highlighted in this brief overview. Suffice it to say that its General Council Meetings are an event in themselves—bringing together, as they do, publishers of diverse backgrounds and experience. The various forums that APNET officials have addressed in different parts of the world have given international exposure to the organization and have helped to spread its message. In just over two years, the APNET story has reached every part of the African continent, Europe, America, and beyond.